Dillon Wallace

The Story Of Grenfell Of The Labrador

© 2025, Dillon Wallace (domaine public)
Publisher : BoD · Books on Demand, 31 avenue Saint-Rémy,
57600 Forbach, bod@bod.fr
Print : Libri Plureos GmbH, Friedensallee 273,
22763 Hamburg (Allemagne)
ISBN : 978-2-3226-2247-4
Dépôt légal : Avril 2025

The Story Of Grenfell Of The Labrador

By
Dillon Wallace

The Story of Grenfell of the Labrador

I
THE SANDS OF DEE

The first great adventure in the life of our hero occurred on the twenty-eighth day of February in the year 1865. He was born that day. The greatest adventure as well as the greatest event that ever comes into anybody's life is the adventure of being born.

If there is such a thing as luck, Wilfred Thomason Grenfell, as his parents named him, fell into luck, when he was born on February twenty-eighth, 1865. He might have been born on February twenty-ninth one year earlier, and that would have been little short of a catastrophe, for in that case his birthdays would have been separated by intervals of four years, and every boy knows what a hardship it would be to wait four years for a birthday, when every one else is having one every year. There are people, to be sure, who would like their birthdays to be four years apart, but they are not boys.

Grenfell was also lucky, or, let us say, fortunate in the place where he was born and spent his early boyhood. His father was Head Master of Mostyn House, a school for boys at Parkgate, England, a little fishing village not far from the historic old city of Chester. By referring to your map you will find Chester a dozen miles or so to the southward of Liverpool, though you may not find Parkgate, for it is so small a village that the map makers are quite likely to overlook it.

Here at Parkgate the River Dee flows down into an estuary that opens out into the Irish Sea, and here spread the famous "Sands of Dee," known the world over through Charles Kingsley's pathetic poem, which we have all read, and over which, I confess, I shed tears when a boy:

O Mary, go and call the cattle home,

And call the cattle home,

And call the cattle home,

Across the Sands o' Dee;

The western wind was wild and dank wi' foam,

And all alone went she.

The creeping tide came up along the sand,

And o'er and o'er the sand,

And round and round the sand,

As far as eye could see;

The blinding mist came down and hid the land—

And never home came she.

Oh is it weed, or fish, or floating hair—

A tress o' golden hair,

O' drown'ed maiden's hair,

Above the nets at sea?

Was never salmon yet that shone so fair,

Among the stakes on Dee.

They rowed her in across the rolling foam,

The cruel, crawling foam,

The cruel, hungry foam,

To her grave beside the sea;

But still the boatmen hear her call the cattle home,

Across the Sands o' Dee.

They rowed her in across the rolling foam,The cruel, crawling foam,The cruel, hungry foam,To her grave beside the sea;But still the boatmen hear her call the cattle home,Across the Sands o' Dee.

Charles Kingsley and the poem become nearer and dearer to us than ever with the knowledge that he was a cousin of Grenfell, and knew the Sands o' Dee, over which Grenfell tramped and hunted as a boy, for the sandy plain was close by his father's house.

There was a time when the estuary was a wide deep harbor, and really a part of Liverpool Bay, and great ships from all over the world came into it and sailed up to Chester, which in those days was a famous port. But as years passed the sands, loosened by floods and carried down by the river current, choked and blocked the harbor, and before Grenfell was born it had become so shallow that only fishing vessels and small craft could use it.

Parkgate is on the northern side of the River Dee. On the southern side and beyond the Sands of Dee, rise the green hills of Wales, melting away into blue mysterious distance. Near as Wales is the people over there speak a different tongue from the English, and to young Grenfell and his companions it was a strange and foreign land and the people a strange and mysterious people. We have most of us, in our young days perhaps, thought that all Welshmen were like Taffy, of whom Mother Goose sings:

"Taffy was a Welshman, Taffy was a thief,

Taffy came to my house and stole a piece of beef;

I went to Taffy's house, Taffy wasn't home,

Taffy came to my house and stole a marrow bone;

I went to Taffy's house, Taffy was in bed,

I took the marrow-bone, and beat about his head."

But it was Grenfell's privilege, living so near, to make little visits over into Wales, and he early had an opportunity to learn that Taffy was not in the least like Welshmen. He found them fine, honest, kind-hearted folk, with no more Taffys among them than there are among the English or Americans. The great Lloyd George, perhaps the greatest of living statesmen, is a Welshman, and by him and not by Taffy, we are now measuring the worth of this people who were the near neighbors of Grenfell in his young days.

Mostyn House, where Grenfell lived, overlooked the estuary. From the windows of his father's house he could see the fishing smacks going out upon the great adventurous sea and coming back laden with fish.

Living by the sea where he heard the roar of the breakers and every day smelled the good salt breath of the ocean, it was natural that he should love it, and to learn, almost as soon as he could run about, to row and sail a boat, and to swim and take part in all sorts of water sports. Time and again he went with the fishermen and spent the night and the day with them out upon the sea. This is why it was fortunate that he was born at Parkgate, for his life there as a boy trained him to meet adventures fearlessly and prepared him for the later years which were destined to be years of adventure.

Far up the river, wide marshes reached; and over these marshes, and the Sands of Dee, Grenfell roamed at will. His father and mother were usually away during the long holidays when school was closed, and he and his brothers were left at these times with a vast deal of freedom to do as they pleased and seek the adventure that every boy loves, and on the sands and in the marshes there was always adventure enough to be found.

Shooting in the marshes and out upon the sands was a favorite sport, and when not with the fishermen Grenfell was usually to be found with his gun stalking curlew, oyster diggers, or some other of the numerous birds that frequented the marshes and shores. Barefooted, until the weather grew too cold in autumn, and wearing barely enough clothing to cover his nakedness, he would set out in early morning and not return until night fell.

As often as not he returned from his day's hunting empty handed so far as game was concerned, but this in no wise detracted from the pleasure of the hunt. Game was always worth the getting, but the great joy was in being out of doors and in tramping over the wide flats. With all the freedom given him to hunt, he early learned that no animals or birds were to be killed on any account save for food or purposes of study. This is the rule of every true sportsman. Grenfell has always been a great hunter and a fine shot, but he has never killed needlessly.

Young Grenfell through these expeditions soon learned to take a great deal of interest in the habits of birds and their life history. This led him to try his skill at skinning and mounting specimens. An old fisherman living near his home was an excellent hand at this and gave him his first lessons, and presently he developed into a really expert taxidermist, while his brother made the cases in which he mounted and exhibited his specimens.

His interest in birds excited an interest in flowers and plants and finally in moths and butterflies. The taste for nature study is like the taste for olives. You have to cultivate it, and once the taste is acquired you become extremely fond of it. Grenfell became a student of moths and butterflies. He captured, mounted and identified specimens. He was out of nights with his net hunting them and "sugaring" trees to attract them, and he even bred them. A fine collection was the result, and this, together with one of flowers and plants, was added to that of his mounted birds. In the course of time he had accumulated a creditable museum of natural history, which to this day may be seen at Mostyn House, in Parkgate; and to it have been added specimens of caribou, seals, foxes, porcupines and other Labrador animals, which in his busy later years he has found time to mount, for he is still the same eager and devoted student of nature.

During these early years, with odds and ends of boards that they collected, Grenfell and his brother built a boat to supply a better means of stealing upon flocks of water birds. It was a curious flat-bottomed affair with square ends and resembled a scow more than a rowboat, but it served its purpose well enough, and was doubtless the first craft which the young adventurer, later to become a master mariner, ever commanded. Up and down the estuary, venturing even to the sea, the two lads cruised in their clumsy craft, stopping over night with the kind-hearted fishermen or "sleeping out" when they found themselves too far from home. Many a fine time the ugly little boat gave them until finally it capsized one day leaving them to swim for it and reach the shore as best they could.

At the age of fourteen Grenfell was sent to Marlborough "College," where he had earned a scholarship. This was not a college as we speak of a college in America, but a large university preparatory school.

In the beginning he had a fight with an "old boy," and being victor firmly established his place among his fellow students. Whether at Mostyn House, or later at Marlborough College, Grenfell learned early to use the gloves. It was quite natural, devoted as he was to athletics, that he should become a fine boxer. To this day he loves the sport, and is always ready to put on the gloves for a bout, and it is a mighty good man that can stand up before him. In most boys' schools of that day, and doubtless at Marlborough College, boys settled their differences with gloves, and in all probability Grenfell had plenty of practice, for he was never a mollycoddle. He was perhaps not always the winner, but he was always a true sportsman. There is a vast difference between a "sportsman" and a "sport." Grenfell was a sportsman, never a sport. His life in the open taught him to accept success modestly or failure smilingly, and all through his life he has been a sportsman of high type.

The three years that Grenfell spent at Marlborough College were active ones. He not only made good grades in his studies but he took a leading part in all athletics. Study was easy for him, and this made it possible to devote much time to physical work. Not only did he become an expert boxer, but he had no difficulty in making the school teams, in football, cricket, and other sports that demanded skill, nerve and physical energy.

Like all youngsters running over with the joy of youth and life, he got into his full share of scrapes. If there was anything on foot, mischievous or otherwise, Grenfell was on hand, though his mischief and escapades were all innocent pranks or evasion of rules, such as going out of bounds at prohibited hours to secure goodies. The greater the element of adventure the keener he was for an enterprise. He was not by any means always caught in his pranks, but when he was he admitted his guilt with heroic candor, and like a hero stood up for his punishment. Those were the days when the hickory switch in America, and the cane in England, were the chief instruments of torture.

With the end of his course at Marlborough College, Grenfell was confronted with the momentous question of his future and what he was to do in life. This is a serious question for any young fellow to answer. It is a question that involves one's whole life. Upon the decision rests to a large degree happiness or unhappiness, content or discontent, success or failure.

It impressed him now as a question that demanded his most serious thought. For the first time there came to him a full realization that some day he would have to earn his way in the world with his own brain and hands. A vista of the future years with their responsibilities, lay before him as a reality, and he decided that it was up to him to make the most of those years and to make a success of life. No doubt this realization fell upon him as a shock, as it does upon most lads whose parents have supplied their every need. Now he was called upon to decide the matter for himself, and his future education was to be guided by his choice.

At various periods of his youthful career nearly every boy has an ambition to be an Indian fighter, or a pirate, or a locomotive engineer, or a fireman and save people from burning buildings at the risk of his own life, or to be a hunter of ferocious wild animals. Grenfell had dreamed of a romantic and adventurous career. Now he realized that these ambitions must give place to a sedate profession that would earn him a living and in which he would be contented.

All of his people had been literary workers, educators, clergymen, or officers in the army or navy. There was Charles Kingsley and "Westward Ho." There was Sir Richard Grenvil, immortalized by Tennyson in "The Revenge." There was his own dear grandfather who was a master at Rugby under the great Arnold, whom everybody knows through "Tom Brown at Rugby."

It was the wish of some of his friends and family that he become a clergyman. This did not in the least suit his tastes, and he immediately decided that whatever profession he might choose, it would not be the ministry. The ministry was distasteful to him as a profession, and he had no desire or intention to follow in the footsteps of his ancestors. He wished to be original, and to blaze a new trail for himself.

Grenfell was exceedingly fond of the family physician, and one day he went to him to discuss his problem. This physician had a large practice. He kept several horses to take him about the country visiting his patients, and in his daily rounds he traveled many miles. This was appealing to one who had lived so much out of doors as Grenfell had. As a doctor he, too, could drive about the country visiting patients. He could enjoy the sunshine and feel the drive of rain and wind in his face. He rebelled at the thought of engaging in any profession that would rob him of the open sky. But he also demanded that the profession he should choose should be one of creative work. This would be necessary if his life were to be happy and successful.

Observing the old doctor jogging along the country roads visiting his far-scattered patients, it occurred to Grenfell that here was not only a pleasant but a useful profession. With his knowledge of medicine the doctor assisted nature in restoring people to health. Man must have a well body if he would be happy and useful. Without a well body man's hands would be idle and his brain dull. Only healthy men could invent and build and administer. It was the doctor's job to keep them fit. Here then was creative work of the highest kind! The thought thrilled him!

Every boy of the right sort yearns to be of the greatest possible use in the world. Unselfishness is a natural instinct. Boys are not born selfish. They grow selfish because of association or training, and because they see others about them practicing selfishness. Grenfell's whole training had been toward unselfishness and usefulness. Here was a life calling that promised both unselfish and useful service and at the same time would gratify his desire to be a great deal out of doors, and he decided at once that he would study medicine and be a doctor.

His father was pleased with the decision. His course at Marlborough College was completed, and he immediately took special work preparatory to entering London Hospital and University.

In the University he did well. He passed his examinations creditably at the College of Physicians and Surgeons and at London University, and had time to take a most active part in the University athletics as a member of various 'Varsity teams. At one time or another he was secretary of the cricket, football and rowing clubs, and he took part in several famous championship games, and during one term that he was in residence at Oxford University he played on the University football team.

One evening in 1885 Grenfell, largely through curiosity, dropped into a tent where evangelistic meetings were in progress. The evangelists conducting the meeting happened to be the then famous D.L. Moody and Ira D. Sankey. Both Mr. Moody and Mr. Sankey were men of marvelous power and magnetism. Moody was big, wholesome and practical. He preached a religion of smiles and happiness and helpfulness. He lived what he preached. There was no humbug or hypocrisy in him. Sankey never had a peer as a leader of mass singing.

Moody was announcing a hymn when Grenfell entered. Sankey, in his illimitable style, struck up the music. In a moment the vast audience was singing as Grenfell had never heard an audience sing before. After the hymn Moody spoke. Grenfell told me once that that sermon changed his whole outlook upon life. He realized that he was a Christian in name only and not in fact. His religious life was a fraud.

There and then he determined that he must be either an out and out Christian or honestly renounce Christianity. With his home training and teachings he could not do the latter. He decided upon a Christian life. He would do nothing as a doctor that he could not do with a clear conscience as a Christian gentleman. This he also decided: a man's religion is something for him to be proud of and any one ashamed to acknowledge the faith of his fathers is a moral coward, and a moral coward is more contemptible than a physical coward. He also was convinced that a boy or man afraid or ashamed to acknowledge his religious belief could only be a mental weakling.

It was characteristic of Grenfell that whatever he attempted to do he did with courage and enthusiasm. He never was a slacker. The hospital to which he was attached was situated in the centre of the worst slums of London. It occurred to him that he might help the boys, and he secured a room, fitted it up as a gymnasium, and established a sort of boys' club, where on Sundays he held a Bible study class and where he gave the boys physical work on Saturdays. There was no Y.M.C.A. in England at that time where they could enjoy these privileges. In the beginning, there were young thugs who attempted to make trouble. He simply pitched them out, and in the end they were glad enough to return and behave themselves.

Grenfell and his brother, with one of their friends, spent the long holidays when college was closed cruising along the coast in an old fishing smack which they rented. In the course of his cruising, the thought came to him that it was hardly fair to the boys in the slums to run away from them and enjoy himself in the open while they sweltered in the streets, and he began at once to plan a camp for the boys.

This was long before the days of Boy Scouts and their camps. It was before the days of any boys' camps in England. It was an original idea with him that a summer camp would be a fine experience for his boys. At his own expense he established such a camp on the Welsh coast, and during every summer until he finished his studies in the University he took his boys out of the city and gave them a fine outing during a part of the summer holiday period. It was just at this time that the first boys' camp in America was founded by Chief Dudley as an experiment, now the famous Camp Dudley on Lake Champlain. We may therefore consider Grenfell as one of the pioneers in making popular the boys' camp idea, and every boy that has a good time in a summer camp should thank him.

But a time comes when all things must end, good as well as bad, and the time came when Grenfell received his degree and graduated a full-fledged doctor, and a good one, too, we may be sure. Now he was to face the world, and earn his own bread and butter. Pleasant holidays, and boys' camps were behind him. The big work of life, which every boy loves to tackle, was before him.

Then it was that Dr. Frederick Treves, later Sir Frederick, a famous surgeon under whom he had studied, made a suggestion that was to shape young Dr. Grenfell's destiny and make his name known wherever the English tongue is spoken.

II
THE NORTH SEA FLEETS

The North Sea, big as it is, has no great depth. Geologists say that not long ago, as geologists calculate time, its bottom was dry land and connected the British Isles with the continent of Europe. Then it began to sink until the water swept in and covered it, and it is still sinking. The deepest point in the North Sea is not more than thirty fathoms, or one hundred eighty feet. There are areas where it is not over five fathoms deep, and the larger part of it is less than twenty fathoms.

Fish are attracted to the North Sea because it is shallow. Its bottom forms an extensive fishing "bank," we might say, though it is not, properly speaking, a bank at all, and here is found some of the finest fishing in the world.

From time immemorial fishing fleets have gone to the North Sea, and the North Sea fisheries is one of the important industries of Great Britain. Men are born to it and live their lives on the small fishing craft, and their sons follow them for generation after generation. It is a hazardous calling, and the men of the fleets are brave and hardy fellows.

The fishing fleets keep to the sea in winter as well as in summer, and it is a hard life indeed when decks and rigging are covered with ice, and fierce north winds blow the snow down, and the cold is bitter enough to freeze a man's very blood. Seas run high and rough, which is always the case in shallow waters, and great rollers sweep over the decks of the little craft, which of necessity have small draft and low freeboard.

The fishing fleets were like large villages on the sea. At the time of which we write, and it may be so to this day, fast vessels came daily to collect the fish they caught and to take the catch to market. Once in every three months a vessel was permitted to return to its home port for rest and necessary re-fitting, and then the men of her crew were allowed one day ashore for each week they had spent at sea. Now and again there came to the hospital sick or injured men returned from the fleet on these home-coming vessels.

When Grenfell passed his final examinations in 1886, and was admitted to the College of Physicians and Royal College of Surgeons of England, Sir Frederick Treves suggested that he visit the North Sea fishing fleets and lend his service to the fishermen for a time before entering upon private practice. The great surgeon, himself a lover of the sea and acquainted with Grenfell's inclinations toward an active outdoor life, was also aware that Grenfell was a good sailor.

"Don't go in summer," admonished Sir Frederick. "Go in winter when you can see the life of the men at its hardest and when they have the greatest need of a doctor. Anyhow you'll have some rugged days at sea if you go in winter."

He went on to explain that a few men had become interested in the fishermen of the fleets and had chartered a vessel to go among them to offer diversion in the hope of counteracting to some extent the attraction of the whiskey and rum traders whose vessels sold much liquor to the men and did a vast deal of harm. This vessel was open to the visits of the fishermen. Religious services were held aboard her on Sundays. There was no doctor in the fleet, and the skipper, who had been instructed in ordinary bandaging and in giving simple remedies for temporary relief, rendered first aid to the injured or sick until they could be sent away on some home-bound vessel and placed in a hospital for medical or surgical treatment. Thus a week or sometimes two weeks would elapse before the sufferer could be put under a doctor's care. Because of this long delay many men died who, with prompt attention, would doubtless have lived.

"The men who have fitted out this mission boat would like a young doctor to go with it," concluded Sir Frederick. "Go with them for a little while. You'll find plenty of high sea's adventure, and you'll like it."

In more than one way this suited Grenfell exactly. The opportunity for adventure that such a cruise offered appealed to him strongly, as it would appeal to any real live red-blooded man or boy. It also offered an opportunity to gain practical experience in his profession and at the same time render service to brave men who sadly needed it; and he could lend a hand in fighting the liquor evil among the seamen and thus share in helping to care for their moral, as well as their physical welfare. He had seen much of the evils of the liquor traffic during his student days in London, and he had acquired a wholesome hatred for it. In short, he saw an opportunity to help make the lives of these men happier. That is a high ideal for any one—to do something whenever possible to bring happiness into the lives of others.

This was too good an opportunity to let pass. It offered not only practice in his profession but service for others, and there would be the spice of adventure.

He applied without delay for the post, requesting to go on duty the following January. Whether Sir Frederick Treves said a word for him to the newly founded mission or not, I do not know, but at any rate Grenfell, to his great delight, was accepted, and it is probable the group of big hearted men who were sending the vessel to the fishermen were no less pleased to secure the services of a young doctor of his character.

At last the time came for departure. The mission ship was to sail from Yarmouth. Grenfell had been impatiently awaiting orders to begin his duties, when suddenly he received directions to join his vessel prepared to go to sea at once. Filled with enthusiasm and keen for the adventure he boarded the first train for Yarmouth.

It was a dark and rainy night when he arrived. Searching down among the wharves he found the mission ship tied to her moorings. She proved to be a rather diminutive schooner of the type and class used by the North Sea fishermen, and if the young doctor had pictured a large and commodious vessel he was disappointed. But Grenfell had been accustomed in his boyhood to knocking about with fishermen and now he was quite content with nothing better than fell to the lot of those he was to serve.

The little vessel was neat as wax below deck. The crew were big-hearted, brawny, good-natured fellows, and gave the Doctor a fine welcome. Of course his quarters were small and crowded, but he was bound on a mission and an adventure, and cramped quarters were no obstacle to his enthusiasm. Grenfell was not the sort of man to growl or complain at little inconveniences. He was thinking only of the duties he had assumed and the adventures that were before him.

At last he was on the seas, and his life work, though he did not know it then, had begun.

III

ON THE HIGH SEAS

The skipper of the vessel was a bluff, hearty man of the old school of seamen. At the same time he was a sincere Christian devoted to his duties. At the beginning he made it plain that Grenfell was to have quite enough to do to keep him occupied, not only in his capacity as doctor, but in assisting to conduct afloat a work that in many respects resembled that of our present Young Men's Christian Association ashore.

The mission steamer was now to run across to Ostend, Belgium, where supplies were to be taken aboard before joining the fishing fleets.

It was bitterly cold, and while they lay at Ostend taking on cargo the harbor froze over, and they found themselves so firm and fast in the ice that it became necessary to engage a steamer to go around them to break them loose. At last, cargo loaded and ice smashed, they sailed away from Ostend and pointed their bow towards the great fleets, not again to see land for two full months, save Heligoland and Terschelling in the far distant offing.

The little vessel upon which Grenfell sailed was the first sent to the fisheries by the now famous Mission to Deep-Sea Fishermen; and the young Doctor on her deck, hardly yet realizing all that was expected of him, was destined to do no small part in the development of the splendid service that the Mission has since rendered the fishermen.

On the starboard side of the vessel's bow appeared in bold carved letters the words, "Heal the sick," on the port side of the bow, "Preach the Word."

"Preaching the Word" does not necessarily mean, and did not mean here, getting up into a pulpit for an hour or two and preaching orthodox sermons, sometimes as dry as dead husks, on Sundays. Sometimes just a smile and a cheery greeting is the best sermon in the world, and the finest sort of preaching. Just the example of living honestly and speaking truthfully and always lending a hand to the fellow who is in trouble or discouraged, is a fine sermon, for there is not a man or boy living whose life and actions do not have an influence for good or bad on some one else. We do not always realize this, but it is true.

Grenfell little dreamed of the future that this voyage was to open to him. He knew little or nothing at that time of Labrador or Newfoundland. He had never seen an Eskimo nor an American Indian, unless he had chanced to visit a "wild west" show. He had no other expectation than that he should make a single winter cruise with the mission schooner, and then return to England and settle in some promising locality to the practice of his profession, there to rise to success or fade into hum-drum obscurity, as Providence might will.

The fishermen of the North Sea fleet were as rough and ready as the old buccaneers. They were constantly risking their lives and they had not much regard for their own lives or the lives of others. With them life was cheap. Night and day they faced the dangers of the sea as they worked at the trawls, and when they were not sleeping or working there was no amusement for them. Then they were prone to resort to the grog ships, which hovered around them, and they too often drank a great deal more rum than was good for them. They were reared to a rough and cruel life, these fishermen. Hard punishments were dealt the men by the skippers. It was the way of the sea, as they knew it.

There were more than twenty thousand of these men in the North Sea fleets. Grenfell must have been overwhelmed with the thought that he was to be the only doctor within reach of that great number of men. "Heal the sick"—that was his job!

But he resolved to do much more than that! He was going to "Preach the Word" in smiles and cheering words, and was going to help the men in other ways than with his pill box and surgical bandages. As a doctor he realized how harmful liquor was to them, and he was going to fight the grog ships and do his best to put them out of business. In a word, he was not only going to doctor the men but he was going to help them to live straight, clean lives. He was going to play the game as he had played foot ball or pulled his oar with the winning crew at college. He was going to put into it the best that was in him!

That was the way Grenfell always did everything he undertook. When he had to pummel the "old boy" at Marlborough College he did it the best he knew how. Now he had a big job on his hands. He resolved, figuratively, to pummel the rum ships, and he was already planning and inventing ways that would make the men's lives easier. He went into the thing with his characteristic zeal, determined to make good. It is a mighty fine thing to make good. Any of us can make good if we go at things in the way Grenfell went at them—determined, whatever obstacles arise, not to fail. Grenfell never whined about luck going against him. He made his own luck. That is the mark of every successful and big man.

"There are the fleets," said the skipper one day, pointing out over the bow. "We'll make a round of the fleets, and you'll have a chance to get busy patching the men up."

And he was busy. There came as many patients every day as any young doctor could wish to treat. But that was what Grenfell wanted.

As the skipper suggested, the mission boat made a tour of the fleets, of which there were several, each fleet with its own name and colours and commanded by an Admiral. There were the Columbias, the Rashers, the Great Northerners and many others. It was finally with the Great Northerners that the mission boat took its station.

Grenfell visited among the vessels and made friends among the men, who were like big boys, rough and ready. They were always prepared to go into daring ventures. They never flinched at danger. Few of them had ever enjoyed the privilege of going to school, and none of the men and few of the skippers could write. They could read the compass just as men who cannot read can tell the time of day from the clock. But they had their method of dead reckoning and always appeared to know where they were, even though land had not been sighted for days.

Most of these men had been apprentised to the vessels as boys and had followed the sea all their lives. There were always many apprentised boys on the ships, and these worked without other pay than clothing, food and a little pocket money until they were twenty-one years of age. In many cases they received little consideration from the skippers and sometimes were treated with unnecessary roughness and even cruelty.

From the beginning Doctor Grenfell devoted himself not only to healing the sick, but also to bettering the condition of the fishermen. His skill was applied to the healing of their moral as well as their physical ills. Of necessity their life was a rough and rugged one, but there were opportunities to introduce some pleasure into it and to make it happier in many ways. Here was a strong human call that, from the beginning, Grenfell could not resist.

Using his own influence together with the influence of other good men, necessary funds were raised to meet the expenses of additional mission ships, and additional doctors and workers were sent out. Those selected were not only doctors, but men who were qualified by character and ability to guide the seamen to better and cleaner and more wholesome living. Queen Victoria became interested. The grog ships were finally driven from the sea. Laws were enacted to better conditions upon the fishing vessels that the lives of the fishermen might be easier and happier. In the course of time, as the result of Grenfell's tireless efforts, a marvelous change for the better took place.

Thus the years passed. Dr. Grenfell, who in the beginning had given his services to the Mission for a single winter, still remained. He felt it a duty that he could not desert. The work was hard, and it denied him the private practice and the home life to which he had looked forward so hopefully. He never had the time to drive fine horses about the country as he visited patients. But he had no regrets. He had chosen to accept and share the life of the fishermen on the high seas. It was no less a service to his country and to mankind than the service of the soldier fighting in the trenches. When he saw the need and heard the call he was willing enough to sacrifice personal ambitions that he might help others to become finer, better men, and live nobler happier lives.

Looking back over that period there is no doubt that Doctor Grenfell feels a thousand times repaid for any sacrifices he may have made. It is always that way. When we give up something for the other fellow, or do some fine thing to help him, our pleasure at the happiness we have given him makes us somehow forget ourselves and all we have given up.

And so came the year 1891. It was in that year that a member of the Mission Board returned from a visit to Canada and Newfoundland and reported to the Board great need of work among the Newfoundland fishermen similar to that that had been done by Grenfell in the North Sea.

The members of the Board were stirred by what they heard, and it was decided to send a ship across the Atlantic. It was necessary that the man in command be a doctor understanding the work to be done. It was also necessary that he should be a man of high executive and administrative ability, capable of organizing and carrying it on successfully. The man that has made good is the man always looked for to occupy such a post. Grenfell had made good in the North Sea. His work there indeed had been a brilliant success. He was the one man the Board thought of, and he was asked to go.

He accepted. Here was a new field of work and adventure offering ever greater possibilities than the old, and he never hesitated about it.

He began preparations for the new enterprise at once. The Albert, a little ketch-rigged vessel of ninety-seven tons register, was selected. Iron hatches were put into her, she was sheathed with greenhart to withstand the pressure of ice, and thoroughly refitted. Captain Trevize, a Cornishman, was engaged as skipper. Though Doctor Grenfell was himself a master mariner and thoroughly qualified as a navigator, he had never crossed the Atlantic, and in any case he was to be fully occupied with other duties. There was a crew of eight men including the mate, Skipper Joe White, a famous skipper of the North Sea fleets.

On June 15, 1892, the Albert was towed out of Great Yarmouth Harbor, and that day she spread her sails and set her course westward. The great work of Doctor Grenfell's life was now to begin. All the years of toil on the North Sea had been but an introduction to it and a preparation for it. His little vessel was to carry him to the bleak and desolate coast of Labrador and into the ice fields of the North. He was to meet new and strange people, and he was destined to experience many stirring adventures.

IV
DOWN ON THE LABRADOR

Heavy seas and head winds met the Albert, and she ran in at the Irish port of Cookhaven to await better weather. In a day or two she again spread her canvas, Fastnet Rock, at the south end of Ireland, the last land of the Old World to be seen, was lost to view, and in heavy weather she pointed her bow toward St. Johns, Newfoundland.

Twelve days later, in a thick fog, a huge iceberg loomed suddenly up before them, and the Albert barely missed a collision that might have ended the mission. It was the first iceberg that Doctor Grenfell had ever seen. Presently, and through the following years, they were to become as familiar to him as the trees of the forests.

Four hundred years had passed since Cabot on his voyage of discovery had, in his little caraval, passed over the same course that Grenfell now sailed in the Albert. Nineteen days after Fastnet Rock was lost to view, the shores of Newfoundland rose before them. That was fine sailing for the landfall was made almost exactly opposite St. Johns.

The harbor of St. Johns is like a great bowl. The entrance is a narrow passage between high, beetling cliffs rising on either side. From the sea the city is hidden by hills flanked by the cliffs, and a vessel must enter the narrow gateway and pass nearly through it before the city of St. Johns is seen rising from the water's edge upon sloping hill-sides on the opposite side of the harbor. It is one of the safest as well as most picturesque harbors in the world.

As the Albert approached the entrance Doctor Grenfell and the crew were astonished to see clouds of smoke rising from within and obscuring the sky. As they passed the cliffs waves of scorching air met them.

The city was in flames. Much of it was already in ashes. Stark, blackened chimneys rose where buildings had once stood. Flames were still shooting upward from those as yet but partly consumed. Some of the vessels anchored in the harbor were ablaze. Everything had been destroyed or was still burning. The Colonial public buildings, the fine churches, the great warehouses that had lined the wharves, even the wharves themselves, were smouldering ruins, and scarcely a private house remained. It was a scene of complete and terrible desolation. The fire had even extended to the forests beyond the city, and for weeks afterward continued to rage and carry destruction to quiet, scattered homes of the country.

The cause or origin of the fire no one knew. It had come as a devastating scourge. It had left the beautiful little city a mass of blackened, smoking ruins.

The Newfoundlanders are as fine and brave a people as ever lived. Deep trouble had come to them, but they met it with their characteristic heroism. No one was whining, or wringing his hands, or crying out against God. They were accepting it all as cheerfully as any people can ever accept so sweeping a calamity. Benjamin Franklin said, "God helps them that help themselves." That is as true of a city as it is of a person. That is what the St. Johns people were doing, and already, while the fire still burned, they were making plans to take care of themselves and rebuild their city.

Of course Doctor Grenfell could do little to help with his one small ship, but he did what he could. The officials and the people found time to welcome him and to tell him how glad they were that he was to go to Labrador to heal the sick of their fleets and make the lives of the fishermen and the natives of the northern coast happier and pleasanter.

A pilot was necessary to guide the Albert along the uncharted coast of Labrador. Captain Nicholas Fitzgerald was provided by the Newfoundland government to serve in this capacity. Doctor Grenfell invited Mr. Adolph Neilson, Superintendent of Fisheries for Newfoundland, to accompany them, and he accepted the invitation, that he might lend his aid to getting the work of the mission started. He proved a valuable addition to the party. Then the Albert sailed away to cruise her new field of service.

It will be interesting to turn to a map and see for ourselves the country to which Doctor Grenfell was going. We will find Labrador in the northeastern corner of the North American continent, just as Alaska is in the northwestern corner.

Like Alaska, Labrador is a great peninsula and is nearly, though not quite, so large as Alaska. Some maps will show only a narrow strip along the Atlantic east of the peninsula marked "Labrador." This is incorrect. The whole peninsula, bounded on the south by the Gulf of St. Lawrence and Straits of Belle Isle, the east by the Atlantic Ocean, the north by Hudson Straits, the west by Hudson Bay and James Bay and the Province of Quebec, is included in Labrador. The narrow strip on the east is under the jurisdiction of Newfoundland, while the remainder is owned by Quebec. Newfoundland is the oldest colony of Great Britain. It is not a part of Canada, but has a separate government.

The only people living in the interior of Labrador are a few wandering Indians who live by hunting. There are still large parts of the interior that have never been explored by white men, and of which we know little or no more than was known of America when Columbus discovered the then new world.

The people who live on the coast are white men, half-breeds and Eskimos. None of these ever go far inland, and they live by fishing, hunting, and trapping animals for the fur. Those on the south, as far east as Blanc Sablon, on the straits of Belle Isle, speak French. Eastward from Blanc Sablon and northward to a point a little north of Indian Harbor at the northern side of the entrance of Hamilton Inlet, English is spoken. The language on the remainder of the coast is Eskimo, and nearly all of the people are Eskimos. Once upon a time the Eskimos lived and hunted on the southern coast along the Straits of Belle Isle, but only white people and half-breeds are now found south of Hamilton Inlet.

The Labrador coast from Cape Charles in the south to Cape Chidley in the north is scoured as clean as the paving stones of a street. Naked, desolate, forbidding it lies in a somber mist. In part it is low and ragged but as we pass north it gradually rises into bare slopes and finally in the vicinity of Nachbak Bay high mountains, perpendicular and grey, stand out against the sky.

Behind the storm-scoured rocky islands lie the bays and tickles and runs and at the head of the bays the forest begins, reaching back over rolling hills into the mysterious and unknown regions beyond. There is not one beaten road in all the land. There is no sandy beach, no grassy bank, no green field. Nature has been kind to Labrador, however, in one respect. There are innumerable harbors snugly sheltered behind the islands and well out of reach of the rolling breakers and the wind. There is an old saying down on the Labrador that "from one peril there are two ways of escape to three sheltered places." The ice and fog are always perils but the skippers of the coast appear to hold them in disdain and plunge forward through storm and sea when any navigator on earth would expect to meet disaster. For the most part the coast is uncharted and the skippers, many of whom never saw an instrument of navigation in their life, or at least never owned one, sail by rhyme:

"When Joe Bett's P'int you is abreast,Dane's Rock bears due west.West-nor'west you must steer,'Til Brimstone Head do appear.

"The tickle's narrow, not very wide;The deepest water's on the starboard sideWhen in the harbor you is shot,Four fathoms you has got."

It is an evil coast, with hidden reefs and islands scattered like dust its whole length. "The man who sails the Labrador must know it all like his own back yard—not in sunny weather alone, but in the night, when the headlands are like black clouds ahead, and in the mist, when the noise of breakers tells him all that he may know of his whereabouts. A flash of white in the gray distance, a thud and swish from a hidden place: the one is his beacon, the other his foghorn. It is thus, often, that the Doctor gets along."

Labrador has an Arctic climate in winter. The extreme cold of the country is caused by the Arctic current washing its shores. All winter the ocean is frozen as far as one can see. In June, when the ice breaks away, the great Newfoundland fishing fleet of little schooners sails north to remain until the end of September catching cod, for here are the finest cod fishing grounds in the world.

In 1892 there were nearly twenty-five thousand Newfoundlanders on this fleet. Doctor Grenfell's mission was to aid and assist these deep sea fishermen. In those days there was no doctor with the fleet and none on the whole coast, and any one taken seriously ill or badly injured usually died for lack of medical or surgical care. Of course, Grenfell was also to help the people who lived on the coast, that is, the native inhabitants, who needed him. This service he was giving free.

At this season there is more fog than sunshine in those northern latitudes. It settles in a dense pall over the sea, adding to the dangers of navigation. Now the fog was so thick that they could scarcely see the length of the vessel. On the fourth day out the fog lifted for a brief time, and Cape Bauld the northeasterly point of Newfoundland Island, showed his grim old head, as if to bid them goodbye and to wish them good luck "down on The Labrador." Then they were again swallowed by the fog and plunged into the rough seas where the Straits of Belle Isle meet the wide ocean.

No more land was seen, as they ploughed northward through the fog, until August 4th. This was a Thursday. Like the lifting of a curtain on a stage the fog, all at once, melted away, to reveal a scene of marvellous though rugged beauty. As though touched by a hand of magic, the atmosphere, for so many days dank and thick, suddenly became brilliantly clear and transparent, and the sun shone bright and warm.

Off the port bow lay The Labrador, the great silent peninsula of the north. Doctor Grenfell turned to it with a thrill. Here was the land he had come so far to see! Here he would find the people to whom he was to devote his life work!

There before him lay her scattered islands, her grim and rocky headlands and beetling cliffs, and beyond the islands, rolling away into illimitable blue distances her seared hills and the vast unknown region of her interior, whose mysterious secrets she had kept locked within her heart through all time. Back there, hidden from the world, were numberless lakes and rivers and mountains that no white man had ever seen.

The sea rose and fell in a lazy swell. Not far away a school of whales were playing, now and again spouting geysers of water high into the air. Shoals of caplin gave silver flashes upon the surface of the sea where thousands of the little fish crowded one another to the surface of the water. Countless birds and sea fowl hovered before the face of the cliffs and above the placid sea.

A half hundred icebergs, children of age-old glaciers of the far North, were scattered over the green-blue waters. Some of them were of gigantic proportions and strange outlines. There were hills with lofty summits, marvellous castles, turreted and towered, and majestic cathedrals, their icy pinnacles and spires reaching high above the top-masts of the ship and their polished adamantine surfaces sparkling in the brilliant sunshine and scintillating fire and colour with the wondrous iridescent beauty of mammoth opals.

"There's Domino Run," said the pilot.

"Domino Run? What is that?"

"'Tis a fine deep run behind the islands," explained the pilot. "All the fleets of schooners cruisin' north and south go through Domino Run. There's a fine tidy harbor in there, and we'd be findin' some schooners anchored there now."

"We'll go in and see."

"I think 'twould be well and meet some of the fleet. There's liviyeres in there too. There's some liviyeres handy to most of the harbors on the coast."

"Liveyeres? What are liveyeres?"

"They're the folk that live on the coast all the time,—the whites and half-breeds. Newfoundlanders only come to fish in summer, but liveyeres stay the winter. The shop keepers we calls planters. They're set up by traders that has fishin' places. The liveyeres has their homes up the heads of bays in winter, and when the ice fastens over they trap fur. In the summer they come out to the islands to fish."

Doctor Grenfell had heard all this before, but now as he looked at the dreary desolation of the rocks it seemed almost incredible that children could be born and grow to manhood and womanhood and live their lives here, forever fighting for mere existence, and die at last without ever once knowing the comforts that we who live in kindlier warmer lands enjoy.

Presently a beautiful and splendid harbor opened before the Albert. Several schooners were lying at anchor within the harbor's shelter, and the strange new ship created a vast sensation as she hove to and dropped her anchor among them, and hoisted the blue flag of the Deep Sea Mission.

From masthead after masthead rose flags of greeting. It was a glorious welcome for any visitor to receive. A warmer or more cordial greeting could scarcely have been offered the Governor General himself. It was given with the fine hearty fervour and characteristic hospitality of the Newfoundland fishermen and seamen.

The Albert's anchor chains had scarce ceased to rattle before boats were pulling toward her from every vessel in the harbor. Ships enough sailed down the coast, to be sure, but if they were not fishing vessels they were traders looking to barter for fish, bearing sharp men who drove hard bargains with the fishermen, as we shall see. But here was a different vessel from any of them. Everybody knew that this was not a fisherman, and that she was not a trader. What was her business? What had she come for? What did her blue flag mean? These were questions to which everybody must needs find the answer for himself.

Great was their joy when it was learned that the Albert was a hospital ship with a real doctor aboard come to care for and heal their sick and injured, and that the doctor made no charge for his services or his medicine. This was a big point that went to their hearts, for there was scarce a man among them with any money in his pocket, and if Doctor Grenfell had charged them money they could not have called upon him to help them, for they could not have paid him. But here he was ready to serve them without money and without price. The richest, who were poor enough, and the poorest, could alike have his care and medicine. Here, indeed, was cause to wonder and rejoice.

Many of the fishermen took their families with them to live in little huts at the fishing places during the summer, and to help them prepare the fish for market. Forty or fifty men, women and children were packed, like figs in a box, on some of the schooners, with no other sleeping place than under the deck, on top of the cargo of provisions and salt in the hold, wherever they could find a place big enough to squeeze and stow themselves. Under such conditions there were ailing people enough on the schooners who needed a doctor's care.

The mail boat from St. Johns came once a fortnight, to be sure, and she had a doctor aboard her. But he could only see for a moment the more serious cases, and not all of them, hurriedly leave some medicine and go, and then he would not return to see them again in another two weeks. The mail boat had a schedule to make, and the time given her for the voyage between St. Johns and The Labrador was all too short, and she never reached the northernmost coast.

There were calls enough from the very beginning to keep Doctor Grenfell busy with the sick folk of the schooners. All that day the people came, and it was late that evening when the sick on the schooners had been cared for and the last of the visitors had departed.

Thus, on that first day in this new land, in the Harbor of Domino Run, Doctor Grenfell's life work among the deep sea fishermen of The Labrador began in earnest.

But even yet Doctor Grenfell's day's work was not to end. He was to witness a scene that would sicken his heart and excite his deepest pity. An experience awaited him that was to guide him to new and greater plans and to bigger things than he had yet dreamed of.

For a long while a rickety old rowboat had been lying off from the Albert. A bronzed and bearded man sat alone in the boat, eyeing the strange vessel as though afraid to approach nearer. He was thin and gaunt. The evening was chilly, but he was poorly clad, and his clothing was as ragged and as tattered as his old boat.

Finally, as though fearing to intrude, and not sure of his reception, he hailed the Albert.

V

THE RAGGED MAN IN THE RICKETY BOAT

Grenfell, who had been standing at the rail for some time watching the decrepid old boat and its strange occupant, answered the hail cheerily.

"Be there a doctor aboard, sir?" asked the man.

"Yes," answered Grenfell. "I'm a doctor."

"Us were hearin' now they's a doctor on your vessel," said the man with satisfaction. "Be you a real doctor, sir?"

"Yes," assured the Doctor. "I hope I am."

"They's a man ashore that's wonderful bad off, but us hasn't no money," suggested the man, adding expectantly, "You couldn't come to doctor he now could you, sir?"

"Certainly I will," assured the Doctor. "What's the matter with the man? Do you know?"

"He have a distemper in his chest, sir, and a wonderful bad cough," explained the man.

"All right," said the Doctor. "I'll go at once. How far is it?"

"Right handy, sir," said the man with evident relief.

"Pull alongside and I'll be with you in a jiffy," and the Doctor hurried below for his medicine case.

The man was alongside waiting for him when he returned a few moments later, and he stepped into the rickety old boat. As the liveyere rowed away Grenfell may have thought of his own famous flat-boat that sank with him and his brother in the estuary below Parkgate years before when they were left to swim for it. But in his mental comparison it is probable that the flat-boat, even in her oldest and most decrepid days, would have passed for a rather fine and seaworthy craft in contrast to this rickety old rowboat. The boat kept afloat, however, and presently the liveyere pulled it alongside the gray rock that served for a landing. They stepped out and the guide led the way up the rocks to a lonely and miserable little sod hut. At the door he halted.

"Here we is, sir," he announced. "Step right in. They'll be wonderful glad to see you, sir."

Grenfell entered. Within was a room perhaps twelve by fourteen feet in size. A single small window of pieces of glass patched together was designed to admit light and at the same time to exclude God's good fresh air. The floor was of earth, partially paved with small round stones. Built against the walls were six berths, fashioned after the model of ship's berths, three lower and three upper ones. A broken old stove, with its pipe extending through the roof into a mud protection rising upon the peak outside in lieu of a chimney, made a smoky attempt to heat the place. The lower berths and floor served as seats. There was no furniture.

The walls of the hut were damp. The atmosphere was dank and unwholesome and heavy with the ill-smelling odor of stale seal oil and fish. The place was dirty and as unsanitary and unhealthful as any human habitation could well be.

Six ragged, half-starved little children huddled timidly into a corner upon the entrance of the visitor from the ship and gazed at the Doctor with wide-open frightened eyes. In one of the lower bunks lay the sick man coughing himself to death. At his side a gaunt woman, miserably and scantily clothed, was offering him water in a spoon.

It was evident to the trained eye of the Doctor that the man was fatally ill and could live but a short time. He was a hopeless consumptive, and a hasty examination revealed the fact that he was also suffering from a severe attack of pneumonia.

Doctor Grenfell's big sympathetic heart went out to the poor sufferer and his destitute family. What could he do? How could he help the man in such a place? He might remove him to one of the clean, white hospital cots on the Albert, but it would scarcely serve to make easier the impending death, and the exposure and effort of the transfer might even hasten it. Then, too, the wife and children would be denied the satisfaction of the last moments with the departing soul of the husband and father, for the Albert was to sail at once. The summer was short, and up and down the coast many others were in sore need of the Doctor's care, and delay might cost some of them their lives.

Grenfell sat silently for several minutes observing his patient and asking himself the question: "What can I do for this poor man?" If there had only been a doctor that the man could have called a few days earlier his life, at least might have been prolonged.

There was but one answer to the question. There was nothing to do but leave medicine and give advice and directions for the man's care, and to supply the ill-nourished family much-needed food and perhaps some warmer clothing.

If there were only a hospital on the coast where such cases could be taken and properly treated! If there were only some place where fatherless and orphaned children could be cared for! These were some of the thoughts that crowded upon Doctor Grenfell as he left the hut that evening and was rowed back to the Albert. And in the weeks that followed his mind was filled with plans, for never did the picture of the dying man and helpless little ones fade as he saw it that first day in Domino Run.

Another call to go ashore came that evening, and the Doctor answered it promptly. Again he was guided to a little mud hut, but this had an advantage over the other in that it was well ventilated. The one window which it boasted was an open hole in the side wall with no glass or other covering to exclude the fresh air. There was no stove, and an open fire on the earthen floor supplied warmth, while a large opening in the roof, for there was no chimney, offered an escape for the smoke, an offer of which the smoke did not freely take advantage.

On a wooden bench in a corner of the room a man sat doubled up with pain. Here too was a family consisting of the man's wife and several children.

"What's the trouble?" asked the Doctor.

"I'm wonderful bad with a distemper in my insides, sir," answered the man with a groan.

"Been ill long?"

"Aye, sir, for three weeks."

"We'll see what can be done."

"Thank you, sir."

"We'll patch you up and make you as well as ever in a little while," assured the Doctor after a thorough examination, for this proved to be a curable case.

"That'll be fine, sir."

Medicine was provided, with directions for taking, and, as the Doctor had promised, and as he later learned, the man soon recovered his health and returned to his fishing.

The Albert sailed north. Into every little harbor and settlement she dropped her anchor for a visit. She called at the trading posts of the old Hudson's Bay Company at Cartwright, Rigolet and Davis Inlet and the Moravian Missions among the Eskimos in the North. She was welcomed everywhere, and everywhere Doctor Grenfell found so many sick or injured people that the whole summer long he was kept constantly busy.

The waters of this coast were unknown to him. He knew nothing of their tides or reefs or currents. But with confidence in himself and a courage that was well-nigh reckless, he sought out the people of every little harbor that he might give them the help that he had come to give. If there was too great a hazard for the schooner, he used a whale-boat. Once this whale-boat was blown out to sea, once it was driven upon the rocks, once it capsized with all on board, and before the summer ended it became a complete wreck.

Nine hundred cases were treated, some trivial though perhaps painful enough maladies, others most serious or even hopeless. Here was a tooth to be extracted, there a limb to be amputated,—cases of all kinds and descriptions, with never a doctor to whom the people could turn for relief until Doctor Grenfell providentially appeared.

With all the work, the voyage was one of pleasure. Not only the pleasure of making others happier,—the greatest pleasure any one can know,—but it was a rattling fine adventure finding the way among islands that had never appeared on any map and were still unnamed. It was fine fun, too, cruising deep and magnificent fjords past lofty towering cliffs, and exploring new channels. And there were the Eskimos and their great wolfish dogs, and their primitive manner of living and dressing. It was all interesting and fascinating.

Never, however, since that August night in Domino Run, had the little mud hut, the dying man, the grief-stricken, miserable mother, and the neglected and starving little ones been out of Doctor Grenfell's thoughts, and often enough his big heart had ached for the stricken ones. He had never before witnessed such awful depths of poverty.

In other harbors that he had visited in his northern voyage similar heartrending cases had, to be sure, fallen under his attention. In one harbor he found a poor Eskimo both of whose hands had been blown off by the premature discharge of a gun. For days and days the man had endured indescribable agony. Nothing had been done for him, save to bathe the stubs of his shattered arms in cold water, until Doctor Grenfell appeared, for there was no surgeon to call upon to relieve the sufferer.

Everywhere there was a mute cry for help. The people were in need of doctors and hospitals. They were in need of hospital ships to cruise the coast and visit the sick of the harbors. They were in need of clothing that they were unable to purchase for themselves. They were in great need of some one to devise a way that would help them to free themselves from the ancient truck system that kept them forever hopelessly in debt to the traders.

The case of the man in the little mud hut at Domino Run, however, first suggested to Grenfell the need of these things and the thought that he might do something to bring them about. As a result of this visit, he made, during his northward cruise, a most thorough investigation of the requirements of the coast.

It was early October, and snow covered the ground, when the Albert, sailing south, again entered Domino Run and anchored in the harbor. Grenfell was put ashore and walked up the trail to the hut. The man had long since died and been laid to rest. The wife and children were still there. They had no provisions for the winter, and Grenfell, we may be sure, did all in his power to help them and make them more comfortable.

His plans had crystalized. He had determined upon the course he should take. He would go back to England and exert himself to the utmost to raise funds to build hospitals and to provide additional doctors and nurses for The Labrador. He would return to Labrador himself and give his life and strength and the best that was in him for the rest of his days in an attempt to make these people happier. Grenfell the athlete, the football player, the naturalist, and, above all, the doctor, was ready to answer the human call and to sacrifice his own comfort and ease and worldly possessions to the needs of these people. The man that will freely give his life to relieve the suffering of others represents the highest type of manhood. It is divine. It was characteristic of Grenfell.

And so it came about that the ragged man in the rickety boat who led Doctor Grenfell to the dying man in the mud hut was the indirect means of bringing hospitals and stores and many fine things to The Labrador that the coast had never known before. The ragged man in going for the doctor was simply doing a kindly act, a good turn for a needy neighbor. What magnificent results may come from one little act of kindness! This one laid the foundation for a work whose fame has encircled the world.

VI
OVERBOARD!

When Grenfell set out to do a thing he did it. He never in all his life said, "I will if I can." His motto has always been, "I can if I will." He had determined to plant hospitals on the Labrador coast and to send doctors and nurses there to help the people. When he determined to do a thing there was an end of it. It would be done. A great many people plan to do things, but when they find it is hard to carry out their plans, they give them up. They forget that anything that is worth having is hard to get. If diamonds were as easy to find as pebbles they would be worth no more than pebbles.

That was a hard job that Grenfell had set himself, and he knew it. When you have a hard job to do, the best way is to go at it just as soon as ever you can and work at it as hard as ever you can until it is done. That was Grenfell's way, and as soon as he reached St. Johns he began to start things moving. Someone else might have waited to return to England to make a formal report to the Deep Sea Missions Board, and await the Board's approval. Not so with Grenfell. He knew the Board would approve, and time was valuable.

Down on The Labrador winter begins in earnest in October. Already the fishing fleets had returned from Labrador when the Albertreached St. Johns, and the fishermen had brought with them the news of the Albert's visit to The Labrador and the wonderful things Doctor Grenfell had done in the course of his summer's cruise. Praise of his magnificent work was on everybody's lips. The newspapers, always hungry for startling news, had published articles about it. Doctor Grenfell was hailed as a benefactor. All creeds and classes welcomed and praised him,—fishermen, merchants, politicians. Even the dignified Board of Trade had recorded its praise.

It was November when Grenfell arrived in St. Johns. He immediately waited upon the government officials with the result that His Excellency, the

Governor of the Colony, at once called a meeting in the Government House that Grenfell might present his plans for the future to the people. All the great men of the Colony were there. They listened with interest and were moved with enthusiasm. Some fine things were said, and then with the unanimous vote of the meeting resolutions were passed in commendation of Doctor Grenfell's summer's work and expressing the desire that it might continue and grow in accordance with Doctor Grenfell's plans. The resolutions finally pledged the "co-operation of all classes of this community." Here was an assurance that the whole of the fine old Colony was behind him, and it made Grenfell happy.

But this was not all. It is not the way of Newfoundland people to hold meetings and say fine things and pass high-sounding resolutions and then let the whole matter drop as though they felt they had done their duty. Doctor Grenfell would need something more than fine words and pats on the back if he were to put his plans through successfully, though the fine words helped, too, with their encouragement. He would need the help of men of responsibility who would work with him, and His Excellency, the Governor, recognizing this fact, appointed a committee composed of some of Newfoundland's best men for this purpose.

Then it was that Mr. W. Baine Grieve arose and began to speak. Mr. Grieve was a famous merchant of the Colony, and a member of the firm of Baine Johnston and Company, who owned a large trading station and stores at Battle Harbor, on an island near Cape Charles, at the southeastern extremity of Labrador. He was a man of importance in St. Johns and a leader in the Colony. As he spoke Grenfell suddenly realized that Mr. Grieve was presenting the Mission with a building at Battle Harbor which was to be fitted as a hospital and made ready for use the following summer.

What a thrill must have come to Grenfell at that moment! The whole Newfoundland government was behind him! His first hospital was already assured! We can easily imagine that he was fairly overwhelmed and dazed with the success that he had met so suddenly and unexpectedly.

But Grenfell was not a man to lose his head. This was only a beginning. He must have more hospitals than one. He must have doctors and nurses, medicines and hospital supplies, food and clothing, and a steam vessel that would take him quickly about to see the sick of the harbors. A great deal of money would be required, and when the Albert sailed out of St. John's Harbor and turned back to England he knew that he had assumed a stupendous job, and that the winter was not to be an idle one for him by any means.

It was December first when the Albert reached England. With the backing and assistance of the Mission Board, Doctor Grenfell and Captain Trevize of the Albert arranged a speaking tour for the purpose of exciting interest in the

Labrador work. Men and women were moved by the tale of their experiences and the suffering and needs of the fishermen and liveres. Gifts were made and sufficient funds subscribed to purchase necessary supplies and hospital equipment, and a fine rowboat was donated to replace the Albert's whaleboat which had been smashed during the previous summer.

Then word came from St. Johns that the great shipping firm of Job Brothers, who owned a fisheries' station at Indian Harbor, had donated a hospital to the Newfoundland committee. This was to be erected at Indian Harbor, at the northern side of the entrance to Hamilton Inlet, two hundred miles north of Battle Harbor, and was to be ready for use during the summer. This was fine news. Not only were there large fishery stations at both Battle Harbor and Indian Harbor, but both were regular stopping places for the fishing schooners when going north and again on their homeward voyage. With two hospitals on the coast a splendid beginning for the work would be made.

But there was still one necessity lacking,—a little steamer in which Doctor Grenfell could visit the folk of the scattered harbors. At Chester on the River Dee and not far from his boyhood home at Parkgate Grenfell discovered a boat one day that was for sale and that he believed would answer his purpose. It was a sturdy little steam launch, forty-five feet over all. It was, however, ridiculously narrow, with a beam of only eight feet, and was sure to roll terribly in any sea and even in an ordinary swell.

But Grenfell was a good seaman, and he could make out in a boat that did a bit of tumbling. He was the sort of man to do a good job with a tool that did not suit him if he could not get just the sort of tool he wanted, and never find fault with it either. The necessary amount to purchase the launch was subscribed by a friend of the Mission. Grenfell bought it and was mightily pleased that this last need was filled. Later the little launch was christened the "Princess May."

Then the Albert was made ready for her second voyage to Labrador. The Mission Board appointed two young physicians to accompany Doctor Grenfell, Doctor Arthur O. Bobardt and Doctor Eliott Curwen, and two trained nurses, Miss Cecilia Williams and Miss Ada Cawardine, that there might be a doctor and a nurse for the hospital at Battle Harbor and a doctor and a nurse for the hospital at Indian Harbor. The launch Princess May was swung aboard the big Allan liner Corean and shipped to St. John's, and on June second Doctor Grenfell and his staff sailed from Queenstown on the Albert.

Grenfell was as fond of sports as ever he was in his boyhood and college days, and now, when the weather permitted, he played cricket with any on board who would play with him. The deck of so small a vessel as the Albert offers small space for a game of this sort, and one after another the cricket balls were lost overboard until but one remained. Then, one day, in the midst of a game in mid-ocean, that last ball unceremoniously followed the others into the sea.

Grenfell ran to the rail. He could see the ball rise on a wave astern.

"Tack back and pick me up!" he yelled to the helmsman, and to the astonishment and consternation of everyone, over the rail he dived in pursuit of the ball.

Grenfell could swim like a fish. He learned that in the River Dee and the estuary, when he was a boy, and he always kept himself in athletic training. But he had never before jumped into the middle of so large a swimming pool as the Atlantic ocean, with the nearest land a thousand miles away!

The steersman lost his head. He put over the helm, but failed to cut Grenfell off, and the Doctor presently found himself a long way from the ship struggling for life in the icy cold waters of the North Atlantic.

VII
IN THE BREAKERS

The young adventurer did not lose his head, and he did not waste his strength in desperate efforts to overtake the vessel. He calmly laid-to, kept his head above water, and waited for the helmsman to bring the ship around again.

A man less inured to hardships, or less physically fit, would have surrendered to the icy waters or to fatigue. Grenfell was as fit as ever a man could be.

In school and college he had made a record in athletic sports, and since leaving the university he had not permitted himself to get out of training. An athlete cannot keep in condition who indulges in cigarettes or liquor or otherwise dissipates, and Grenfell had lived clean and straight.

It was this that saved his life now. He knew he was fit and he had confidence in himself, and was unafraid. While he appreciated his peril, he never lost his nerve, and when finally he was rescued and found himself on deck he was little the worse for his experience, and with a change of dry clothing was ready to resume the interrupted game of cricket with the rescued ball.

With no further adventure than once coming to close quarters with an iceberg and escaping without serious damage, the Albert arrived in due time at St. John's, and Grenfell was at once occupied in preparation for his summer's work on The Labrador. Materials with which to construct the Indian Harbor hospital were shipped north by steamer. Supplies were taken aboard the Albert, and with Dr. Curwin and nurses Williams and Cawardine she sailed for Battle Harbor, where the building to be utilized as a hospital was already erected.

Then the launch Princess May, which had been landed from the Corean, was made ready for sea, and with an engineer and a cook as his crew and Dr. Bobardt as a companion, Dr. Grenfell as skipper put to sea in the tiny craft on July 7th.

There were many pessimistic prophets to see the Princess May off. From skipper to cook not a man aboard her was familiar with the coast, or could recognize a single landmark or headland either on the Newfoundland coast or on The Labrador.

They were going into rugged, fog-clogged seas. They might encounter an ice-pack, and the sea was always strewn with menacing icebergs. True, they had charts, but the charts were most incomplete, and no Newfoundlander sails by them.

The Princess May, a mere cockle-shell, was too small, it was said, for the undertaking. She was six years old and Grenfell had not given her a try-out. The consensus of opinion among the wise old Newfoundland seamen who gathered on the wharf as she sailed was that Doctor Grenfell and his crew were much like the three wise men of Gotham who went to sea in a bowl. Still, not a man of them but would have ventured forth upon the high seas in an ancient rotten old hull of a schooner. They were acquainted with schooners and the coast, while the little launch Princess May was a new species of craft to them, and was manned by green hands.

"'Tis a dangerous voyage for green hands to be makin'," said one, "and that small boat were never meant for the sea."

"Aye, for green hands," said another. "They'll never make un without mishap."

"If they does, 'twill be by the mercy o' God."

"And how'll they make harbor, not knowin' what to sail by?"

"That bit of a craft would never stand half a gale, and if she meets th' ice she'll crumple up like an eggshell."

"And they'll be havin' some nasty weather, I says. We'll never hear o' she again or any o' them on board."

"Unless by the mercy o' God."

Such were the remarks of those ashore as the Princess May steamed down the harbor and out through the narrow channel between the beetling cliffs, into the broad Atlantic. Dr. Grenfell has confessed that he was not wholly without misgivings himself, and they seemed well founded when, at the end of the first five miles, the engineer reported:

"She's sprung a leak, sir!" and anxiously asked, "Had we better put back?"

"No! We'll stand on!" answered Grenfell. "Those croakers ashore would never let us hear the end of it if we turned back. We'll see what's happened."

An examination discovered a small opening in the bottom. A wooden plug was shaped and driven into the hole. To Doctor Grenfell's satisfaction and relief, this was found to heal the leak effectually, and the Princess May continued on her course.

But this was not to end the difficulties. In those waters dense fogs settled suddenly and without warning, and now such a fog fell upon them to shut out all view of land and the surrounding sea.

Nevertheless, the Princess May steamed bravely ahead. To avoid danger Grenfell was holding her, as he believed, well out to sea, when suddenly there rose out of the fog a perpendicular towering cliff. They were almost in the white surf of the waves pounding upon the rocky base of the cliff before they were aware of their perilous position.

Every one expected that the little vessel would be driven upon the rocks and lost, and they realized if that were to happen only a miracle could save them. Grenfell shouted to the engineer, the engine was reversed and by skillful maneuvering the Princess Maysucceeded, by the narrowest margin, in escaping unharmed. To their own steady nerves, and the intervention of Providence the fearless mariner and his little crew undoubtedly owed their lives.

Grenfell suspected that the compass was not registering correctly. Standing out to sea until they were at a safe distance from the treacherous shore rocks, a careful examination was made. The binnacle had been left in St. Johns for necessary repairs, and the examination discovered that iron screws had been used to make the compass box fast to the cabin. These screws were responsible for a serious deviation of the needle, and this it was that had so nearly led them to fatal disaster.

A heavy swell was running, and the little vessel, with but eight feet beam, rolled so rapidly that the compass needle, even when the defect had been remedied, made a wide swing from side to side as the vessel rolled. The best that could be done was to read the dial midway between the extreme points of the needle's swing. This was deemed safe enough, and away the Princess May ploughed again through the fog.

At five o'clock in the afternoon it was decided to work in toward shore and search for a sheltering harbor in which to anchor for the night. Under any circumstance it would be foolhardy for so small a vessel to remain in the open sea outside, after darkness set in, in those ice-menaced fog-choked northern waters. The course of the Princess May was accordingly changed to bear to the westward and Grenfell was continuously feeling his way through the fog when suddenly, and to the dismay of all on board, they found themselves surrounded by jagged reefs and small rocky islands and in the midst of boiling surf.

Now they were indeed in grave peril. They must needs maintain sufficient headway to keep the vessel under her helm. Black rocks capped with foam rose on every side, they did not know the depth of the water, and the fog was so thick they could scarce see two boat lengths from her bow.

VIII
AN ADVENTUROUS VOYAGE

The finest school of courage in the world is the open. The Sands of Dee, the estuary and the hills of Wales made a fine school of this sort for Grenfell.

The out-of-doors clears the brain, and there a man learns to think straight and to the point. When he is on intimate terms with the woods and mountains, and can laugh at howling gales and the wind beating in his face, and can take care of himself and be happy without the effeminating comforts of steam heat and luxurious beds, a man will prove himself no coward when he comes some day face to face with grave danger. He has been trained in a school of courage. He has learned to depend upon himself.

Fine, active games of competition like baseball, football, basketball and boxing, give nerve, self-confidence and poise. Through them the hand learns instinctively, and without a moment's hesitation, to do the thing the brain tells it to do.

Down on The Labrador they say that Grenfell has always been "lucky" in getting out of tight places and bad corners. But we all know, 'way down in our hearts, that there is no such thing as "luck." "God helps them that help themselves." That's the secret of Grenfell's getting out of such tight corners as this one that he had now run into in the fog. He was trained in the school of courage. He helped himself, and he knew how. He was unafraid.

So it was now as always afterward. Grim danger was threatening the Princess May on every side. Each moment Grenfell and his companions expected to feel the shock of collision and hear the fatal crunching and splintering of the vessel's timbers upon the rocks. All of Grenfell's experiences on the Sands of Dee and in the hills of Wales and out on the estuary came to his rescue. He did not lose his head for a moment. That would have been fatal. He had acquired courage and resourcefulness in that out-of-door school he had attended when a boy. The situation called for all the grit and good judgment he and his crew possessed.

Under just enough steam to give the vessel steerageway, they wound in and out between protruding rocks and miniature islands amidst the white foam of breakers that pounded upon the rocks all around them. At length they were headed about. Then cautiously they threaded their way into the open sea and safety.

This was to be but an incident in the years of labor that lay before Grenfell on The Labrador. He was to have no end of exciting experiences, some of them so thrilling that this one was, in comparison, to fade into insignificance. Labrador is a land of adventures. The man who casts his lot in that bleak country cannot escape them. Adventure lurks in every cove and harbor, on every turn of the trail, ready to spring out upon you and try your mettle, and learn the sort of stuff you are made of.

Later in the evening they again felt their way landward through the fog. To their delight they presently found themselves in a harbor, and that night they rested in a safe and snug anchorage sheltered from wind and pounding sea.

There was adventure enough on that voyage to satisfy anybody. The sun did not set that the voyagers had not experienced at least one good thrill during the daylight hours. On the seventh day from St. Johns the Princess May crossed the Straits of Belle Isle, and drew alongside the Albert at Battle Harbor.

The new hospital was nearly ready to receive patients, the first of the hospitals to be built as a result of the visit to the Albert the previous summer of the ragged man in the rickety boat. The other hospital was in course of building at Indian Harbor, and Doctor Grenfell dispatched the Albert, with Doctor Curwin and Miss Williams to assist in preparing it for patients, while Doctor Bobart and Miss Cawardine remained in charge of the Battle Harbor hospital.

Away Doctor Grenfell steamed again in the Princess May nothing daunted by his many difficulties with the little craft in his voyage from St. John's. It was necessary that he know the headlands and the harbors, the dangerous places and the safe ones along the whole coast. The only way to do this was by visiting them, and the quickest and best way to learn them was by finding them out for himself while navigating his own craft. Now, light houses stand on two or three of the most dangerous points of the coast, but in those days there were none, and there were no correct charts. The mariner had to carry everything in his head, and indeed he must still do so. He must know the eight hundred miles of coast as we know the nooks and corners of our dooryards.

Doctor Grenfell wished also to make the acquaintance of the people. He wished to visit them in their homes that he might learn their needs and troubles and so know better how to help them. He was not alone to be their doctor. He was to clothe and feed the poor so far as he could and to put them in a way to help themselves.

To do this it was necessary that he know them as a man knows his near neighbors. He must needs know them as the family doctor knows his patients. He was no preacher, but, to some degree, he was to be their pastor and look after their moral as well as their physical welfare. In short, he was to be their friend, and if he were to do his best for them, they would have to look upon him as a friend and not only call upon him when they were in need, but lend him any assistance they could. To this end they would have to be taught to accept him as one of themselves, come to live among them, and not as an occasional visitor or a foreigner.

With the exception of a few small settlements of a half-dozen houses or so in each settlement, the cabins on the Labrador coast are ten or fifteen and often twenty or more miles apart. If all of them were brought together there would scarcely be enough to make one fair-sized village.

All of the people, as we have seen, live on the seacoast, and not inland. Only wandering Indians live in the interior. Though Labrador is nearly as large as Alaska, there is no permanent dwelling in the whole interior. It is a vast, trackless, uninhabited wilderness of stunted forests and wide, naked barrens.

The Liveyeres, as the natives, other than Indians and Eskimos, are called, have no other occupation than trapping and hunting in winter, and fishing in summer. Their winter cabins are at the heads of deep bays, in the edge of the forest. In the summer they move to their fishing places farther down the bays or on scattered, barren islands, where they live in rude huts or, sometimes, in tents. They catch cod chiefly, but also, at the mouths of rivers, salmon and trout. All the fish are salted, and, like the furs caught in winter, bartered totraders for tea and flour and pork and other necessities of life.

To make the acquaintance of these scattered people, along hundreds of miles of coast, was a big undertaking. And then, too, there were the settlements in the north of Newfoundland, among whose people he was to work. Doctor Grenfell, and his assistants were the only doctors that any of them could call upon.

And there were the fishermen of the fleet. The twenty-five thousand or more men, women and children attached to the Newfoundland summer fisheries on The Labrador formed a temporary summer population.

He could not hope, of course, in the two or three months they were there, to get on intimate terms with all of them, but he was to meet as many as he could, and renew and increase both his acquaintances and his service of the year before. With the Princess May to visit the sick folk ashore, and the hospital ship Albert, which was to serve, in a manner, as a sea ambulance to take serious cases to the new hospitals at Indian Harbor and Battle Harbor, Doctor Grenfell felt that he had made a good start.

As already suggested, this was an adventurous voyage. Twice that summer the Princess May went aground on the rocks, and once theAlbert was fastened on a reef. Both vessels lost sections of their keels, but otherwise, due to good seamanship, escaped with minor injuries.

At every place the Doctor visited he made a record of the people. After the names of the poorer and destitute ones was listed the things of which they were most in need.

In one poor little cabin the mother of a large family had, though ill, kept to her duties in and out of the house until she could stand on her feet no longer, and when Doctor Grenfell entered the cabin he found her lying helpless on a rough couch of boards, with scarce enough bed clothing to cover her. Some half-clad children shivered behind a miserable broken stove, which radiated little heat but sent forth much smoke. The haggard and worn out father was walking up and down the chill room with a wee mite of a baby in his arms, while it cried pitifully for food. Like all the family the poor little thing was starving.

The mother was suffering with an acute attack of bronchitis and pleurisy. All were suffering from lack of food and clothing. The children were barefooted. One little fellow had no other covering than an old trouser leg drawn over his frail little body. The man's fur hunt had failed the previous winter. Sickness prevented fishing. There was nothing in the house to eat and the family were helpless. Doctor Grenfell came to them none too soon.

In every harbor and bay and cove there was enough for Doctor Grenfell to do. His heart and hands were full that summer as they have ever been since. His skill was constantly in demand. Here was some one desperately ill, there a finger or an arm to be amputated, or a more serious operation to be performed.

The hospitals were soon filled to overflowing. Doctor Grenfell afloat, and his two assistants with the nurses in the hospitals were busy night and day. The best of it all was many lives were saved. Some who would have been helpless invalids as long as they lived were sent home from the hospitals strong and well and hearty. An instance of this was a girl of fourteen, who had suffered for three years with internal abesses that would eventually have killed her. She was taken to the Battle Harbor Hospital, operated upon, and was soon perfectly well. To this day she is living, a robust contented woman, the mother of a family, and, perchance, a grandmother.

Grenfell was happy. Here was something better than jogging over English highways behind a horse and visiting well-to-do grumbling patients. He was out on the sea he loved, meeting adventure in fog and storm and gale. That was better than a gig on a country road. He was helping people to be happy. He prized that far more than the wealth he might have accumulated, or the reputation he might have gained at home, as a famous physician or surgeon. There is no happiness in the world to compare with the happiness that comes with the knowledge that one is making others happy and helping them to better living and contentment.

Without knowing it, Grenfell was building a world-fame. If he had known it, he would not have cared a straw. He was working not for fame but for results —for the good he could do others. Nothing else has ever influenced him. Every day he was doing endless good turns without pay or the thought of pay. In this he was serving not only God but his country. And he never neglected his athletics, for it was necessary that he keep his body in the finest physical condition that his brain might always be keen and alert. Grenfell could not have remained a year in the field if he had neglected his body, and he was still an athlete in the pink of condition.

IX
IN THE DEEP WILDERNESS

Imagine, if you will, a vast primeval wilderness spreading away before you for hundreds of miles, uninhabited, grim and solitary. None but wild beasts and the roving Indians that hunt them live there. None but they know the mysteries that lie hidden and guarded by those trackless miles of forests and barren reaches of unexplored country.

And so this wilderness has lain since creation, unmarred by the hand of civilized man, clean and unsullied, as God made it. The air, laden with the perfume of spruce and balsam, is pure and wholesome. The water carries no germs from the refuse of man, and one may drink it freely, from river and brook and lake, without fear of contamination. There is no sound to break the silence of ages save the song of river rapids, the thunder of mighty falls, or the whisper or moan of wind in the tree tops; or, perchance, the distant cry of a wolf, the weird laugh of a loon or the honk of the wild goose.

There are no roads or beaten trails other than the trails of the caribou, the wild deer that make this their home. The nearest railroad is half a thousand miles away. Automobiles are unknown and would be quite useless here. Great rivers and innumerable emerald lakes render the land impassable for horses. The traveler must make his own trails, and he must depend in summer upon his canoe or boat, and in winter upon his snowshoes and his sledge, hauled by great wolf dogs.

With his gun and traps and fishing gear he must glean his living from the wilderness or from the sea. If he would have a shelter he must fell trees with his axe and build it with his own skill. He has little that his own hands and brain do not provide. He must be resourceful and self-reliant.

I venture to say there is not a boy living—a real red-blooded boy or red-blooded man either for that matter—who has not dreamed of the day when he might experience the thrill of venturing into such a wilderness as we have described. This was America as the discoverers found it, and as it was before the great explorers and adventurers opened it to civilization. This was Labrador as Grenfell found Labrador, and as it is to-day—the great "silent peninsula of the North." It occupies a large corner of the North American continent, and much of it is still unexplored, a vast, grim, lonely land, but one of majestic grandeur and beauty.

The hardy pioneers and settlers of Labrador, as we have seen, have made their homes only on the seacoast, leaving the interior to wandering Indian hunters. They do, to be sure, enter the wilderness for short distances in winter when they are following their business as hunters, but none has ever made his home beyond the sound of the sea.

In the forests of the south and southeast are the Mountaineer Indians, as they are called by all English speaking people; or, if we wish to put on airs and assume French we may call them the Montaignais Indians. In the North are the Nascaupees, today the most primitive Indians on the North American continent. In the west and southwest are the Crees.

All of these Indians are of the great Algonquin family, and are much like those that Natty Bumpo chummed with or fought against, and those who lived in New York and New England when the settlers first came to what are now our eastern states. Labrador is so large, and there are so few Indians to occupy it, however, that the explorer may wander through it for months, as I have done, without ever once seeing the smoke rising from an Indian tepee or hearing a human voice.

The Eskimos of the north coast are much like the Eskimos of Greenland, both in language and in the way they live. Their summer shelters are skin tents, which they call tupeks. In winter they build dome-shaped houses from blocks of snow, though they sometimes have cave-like shelters of stone and earth built against the side of a hill. The snow houses they call iglooweuks, or houses of snow; the stone and earth shelters are igloosoaks, or big igloos, the word igloo, in the Eskimo language, meaning house. When winter comes big snow drifts soon cover the igloosoaks, and the snow keeps out the wind and cold. As a further protection, snow tunnels, through which the people crawl on hands and knees, are built out from the entrance to the igloosoak, and these keep all drafts, when a gale blows, from those within.

The Eskimos heat their snow igloos, and in treeless regions their igloosoaks also, with lamps of hollowed stone. These lamps are made in the form of a half moon. Seal oil is used as fuel, and a rag, if there is any to be had, or moss, resting upon the straight side of the lamp, does service as the wick.

Of course the snow igloos must never be permitted to get so warm that the snow will melt. The temperature in a snow house is therefore kept at about thirty degrees, or a little lower. Nevertheless it is comfortable enough, when the temperature outside is perhaps forty or fifty degrees below zero and quite likely a stiff breeze blowing. Comfort is always a matter of comparison. I have spent a good many nights in snow houses, and was always glad to enjoy the comfort they offered. To the traveler who has been in the open all day, the snow house is a cozy retreat and a snug enough place to rest and sleep in.

On the east coast the Eskimos are more civilized and live much like the liveyeres. All Eskimos are kind hearted, hospitable people. Once, I remember, when an Eskimo host noticed that the bottom of my sealskin mocasins had worn through to the stocking, he pulled those he wore off his feet, and insisted upon me wearing them. He had others, to be sure, but they were not so good as those he gave me. No matter how poorly off he is, an Eskimo will feel quite offended if a visitor does not share with him what he has to eat.

Though Dr. Grenfell's hospitals are farther south, on the coast where the liveyeres have their cabins, he cruises northward to the Eskimo country of the east coast every summer, and in the summer has nursing stations there. Sometimes, when there is a case demanding it, he brings the sick Eskimos to one of the hospitals. But, generally, the east coast Eskimos are looked after by the Moravian Brethren in their missions, and in summer Dr. Grenfell calls at the missions to give them his medical and surgical assistance.

As stated before, the liveyeres and others than the Indians, build their cabins on the coast, usually on the shores of bays, but always by the salt water and where they can hear the sound of the sea. Every man of them is a hunter or a fisherman or both, and the boys grow up with guns in their hands, and pulling at an oar or sailing a boat. They begin as soon as they can walk to learn the ways of the wilderness and of the wild things that live in it, and they are good sailors and know a great deal about the sea and the fish while they are still wee lads. That is to be their profession, and they are preparing for it.

The Labrador home of the liveyere usually contains two rooms, but occasionally three, though there are many, especially north of Hamilton Inlet, of but a single room. All have an enclosed lean-to porch at the entrance. This serves not only as a protection from drifting snow in winter, but as a place where stovewood is piled, dog harness and snowshoes are hung, and various articles stored.

In the cabin is a large wood-burning stove, the first and most important piece of furniture. There is a home-made table and sometimes a home-made chair or two, though usually chests in which clothing and furs are stored are utilized also as seats. A closet built at one side holds the meager supply of dishes. On a mantelshelf the clock ticks, if the cabin boasts one, and by its side rests a well-thumbed Bible.

Bunks, built against the rear of the room, serve as beds. If there is a second room, it supplies additional sleeping quarters, with bunks built against the walls as in the living room. Travelers and visitors carry their own sleeping bags and bedding with them and sleep upon the floor. This is the sort of bed Dr. Grenfell enjoys when sleeping at night in a liveyere's home.

On the beams overhead are rifles and shotguns, always within easy reach, for a shot at some game may offer at any time. The side walls of the cabins are papered with old newspapers, or illustrations cut from old magazines.

The more thrifty and cleanly scrub floors, tables, doors and all woodwork with soap and sand once a week, until everything is spotlessly clean. But along the coast one comes upon cabins often enough that appear never to have had a cleaning day, and in which the odor of seal oil and fish is heavy.

Those of the Newfoundland fishermen that bring their families to the coast live in all sorts of cabins. Some are well built and comfortable, while others are merely sod-covered huts with earthen floor. These are occupied, however, only during the fishing season. The fishermen move into them early in July and begin to leave them early in September.

As stated elsewhere, no farming can be done in Labrador, and the only way men can make a living is by hunting and fishing. Eskimos seldom venture far inland on their hunting and trapping expeditions, but some of the liveyeres go fifty or sixty miles from the coast to set their traps, and some of those in Hamilton Inlet go up the Grand River for a distance of more than two hundred and fifty miles, and others go up the Nascaupee River for upwards of a hundred miles.

Trapping is all done in winter and it is a lonely and adventurous calling. Early in September, the men who go the greatest distance inland set out for their trapping grounds. Usually two men go together. They build a small log hut called a "tilt," about eight by ten feet in size. Against each of two sides a bunk is made of saplings and covered with spruce or balsam boughs. On the boughs the sleeping bags are spread, and the result is a comfortable bed. The bunks also serve as seats. A little sheet iron stove that weighs, including stovepipe, about eighteen pounds and is easy to transport, heats the tilt, and answers very well for the trapper's simple cooking. The stovepipe, protruding through the roof, serves as a chimney.

The main tilt is used as a base of supplies, and here reserve provisions are stored together with accumulations of furs as they are caught. Fat salt pork, flour, baking powder or soda, salt, tea and Barbadoes molasses complete the list of provisions carried into the wilderness from the trading post. Other provisions must be hunted.

Each man provides himself with a frying pan, a tin cup, a spoon or two, a tin pail to serve as a tea kettle and sometimes a slightly larger pail for cooking. On his belt he carries a sheath knife, which he uses for cooking, skinning, eating and general utility. He rarely encumbers himself with a fork.

For use on the trail each man has a stove similar to the one that heats the tilt, a small cotton tent, and a toboggan.

From the base tilt the trapping paths or trails lead out. Each trapper has a path which he has established and which he works alone. He hauls his sleeping bag, provisions and other equipment on his toboggan or, as he calls it, "flat sled." He carries his rifle in his hand and his ax is stowed on the toboggan, for he never knows when a quick shot will get him a pelt or a day's food.

Sometimes tilts are built along the path at the end of a day's journey, but if there is no tilt the cotton tent is pitched. In likely places traps are set for marten, mink or fox. Ice prevents trapping for the otter in winter, but they are often shot.

At the end of a week or fortnight the partners meet at the base tilt. Otherwise each man is alone, and we may imagine how glad they are to see each other when the meeting time comes. But they cannot be idle. Out through the snow-covered forest, along the shores of frozen lakes and on wide bleak marshes the trapper has one hundred traps at least, and some of them as many as three hundred. The men must keep busy to look after them properly, and so, after a Sunday's rest together they again separate and are away on their snowshoes hauling their toboggans after them.

At Christmas time they go back to their homes, down by the sea, to see their wives and children and to make merry for a week. What a meeting that always is! How eagerly the little ones have been looking forward to the day when Daddy would come! O, that blessed Christmas week! But it is only seven days long, and on the second day of January the trappers are away again to their tilts and trails and traps. Again early in March they visit their homes for another week, and then again return to the deep wilderness to remain there until June.

Sometimes the father never comes back, and then the wilderness carries in its heart the secret of his end. Then, oh, those hours of happy expectancy that become days of grave anxiety and finally weeks of black despair! Such a case happened once when I was in Labrador. Later they found the young trapper's body where the man had perished, seventy miles from his home.

As I have said, the life of the trapper is filled with adventure. Many a narrow escape he has, but he never loses his grit. He cannot afford to. Gilbert Blake was one of four trappers that rescued me several years ago, when I had been on short rations in the wilderness for several weeks, and without food for two weeks. I had eaten my moccasins, my feet were frozen and I was so weak I could not walk. Gilbert and I have been friends since then and we later traveled the wilderness together. Gilbert has no trapping partner. His "path" is a hundred miles inland from his home. All winter, with no other companion than a little dog, he works alone in that lonely wilderness.

One winter game was scarce, and Gilbert's provisions were practically exhausted when he set out to strike up his traps preparatory to his visit home in March. He was several miles from his tilt when suddenly one of his snowshoes broke beyond repair. He could not move a step without snowshoes, for the snow lay ten feet deep. He had no skin with him with which to net another snowshoe, even if he were to make the frame; and he had nothing to eat.

A Labrador blizzard came on, and Gilbert for three days was held prisoner in his tent. He spent his time trying to make a serviceable snowshoe with netting woven from parts of his clothing torn into strips. When at last the storm ended and he struck his tent he was famished.

Packing his things on his toboggan he set out for the tilt, but had gone only a short distance when the improvised snowshoe broke. He made repeated efforts to mend it, but always it broke after a few steps forward. He was in a desperate situation.

He had now been nearly three days without eating. He was still several miles from the tilt where he had a scant supply that had been reserved for his journey home. To proceed to the tilt was obviously impossible, and he could only perish by remaining where he was.

Utterly exhausted after a fruitless effort to flounder forward, he sat down upon his flatsled, and looked out over the silent snow waste. Weakened with hunger, it seemed to him that he had reached the end of his endurance. So far as he knew there was not another human being within a hundred miles of where he sat, and he had no expectation or slightest hope of any one coming to his assistance. "I was scrammed," said he, which meant, in our vernacular, he was "all in."

Gilbert is a fine Christian man, and all the time, as he told me in relating his experience, he had been praying God to show him a way to safety. He never was a coward, and he was not afraid to die, for he had faced death many times before and men of the wilderness become accustomed to the thought that sometime, out there in the silence and alone, the hand of the grim messenger may grasp them. But he was afraid for Mrs. Blake and the four little ones at home. Were he to perish there would be no one to earn a living for them. He was frightened to think of the privations those he loved would suffer.

Suddenly, in the distance, he glimpsed two objects moving over the snow. As they came nearer he discovered that they were men. He shouted and waved his arms, and there was an answering signal. Presently two Mountaineer Indians approached, hauling loaded toboggans, laughing and shouting a greeting as they recognized him.

"'Twas an answer to my prayers," said Gilbert in relating the incident to me. "I was fair scrammed when I saw them Indians. They were the first Indians I had seen the whole winter. They weren't pretty, but just then they looked to me like angels from heaven, and just as pretty as any angels could look."

The Indians had recently made a killing, and their toboggans were loaded with fresh caribou meat. They made Gilbert eat until they nearly killed him with kindness, and they had an extra pair of snowshoes, which they gave him.

This is the life of the trapper on The Labrador. This is the sort of man he is— hardy, patient, brave and reverent. He is a man of grit and daring, as he must be to cheerfully meet, with a stout heart and a smile, the constant hardships and adventures that beset him.

Dr. Grenfell declares that it is no hardship to devote his life to helping men like this. His work among them brings constant joy to him. They appreciate him, and he has grown to look upon them as all members of his big family. He takes a personal and devoted interest in each. It is a great comfort to the men to know that if any are sick or injured at home while they are away on the trails the mission doctor will do his best to heal them. Before Grenfell went to The Labrador there was no doctor to call upon the whole winter through.

The trapping season for fur ends in April. Then the trapper "strikes up" his traps, hangs them in trees where he will find them the following fall, packs his belongings on his toboggan and returns home, unless he is to remain to hunt bear. In that case he must wait for the bears to come forth from their winter's sleep, and this will keep the hunter in the wilderness until after the "break-up" comes and the ice goes out. Those who go far inland usually wait in any case until the ice is out of the streams and boat or canoe traveling is possible and safe.

The break-up sets in, usually, early in June. Then come torrential rains. The snow-covered wilderness is transformed into a sea of slush. New brooks rise everywhere and pour down with rush and roar into lakes and rivers. The rivers over-flow their banks. Trees are uprooted and are swept forward on the flood. Broken ice jams and pounds its way through the rapids with sound like thunder. The spring break-up is an inspiring and wonderful spectacle.

When the hunting season ends and the trappers return from their winter trails, they enjoy a respite at home mending fishing nets, repairing boats and making things tidy and ship-shape for the summer's fishing. Everyone is now looking forward with keen anticipation to the first run of fish. From the time the ice goes out all one hears along the coast is talk of fish. "Any signs of fish, b'y?"

One hears it everywhere, for everybody is asking everybody else that question.

In Hamilton Inlet and Sandwich Bay salmon fisheries are of chief importance. Salmon here are all salted down in barrels and not tinned, as on the Pacific coast. Once there was a salmon cannery in Sandwich Bay, but the Hudson's Bay Company bought it and demolished it, as there was doubtless less work and more profit for the Company in salted salmon. Elsewhere the fisheries are mainly for cod.

In a frontier land it is not easy to earn a living. Everybody must work hard all the time. Men, women, boys and girls all do their share at the fishing. Women and children help to split and cure the fish. It is a proud day for any lad when he is big enough and strong enough to pull a stroke with the heavy oar, and go out to sea with his father.

The Labrador, or Arctic, current now and again keeps ice drifting along the coast the whole summer through. When ice is there fishermen cannot set their nets and fish traps, for the ice would tear the gear and ruin it. Neither can they fish successfully with hook and line when the ice is in. When this happens few fish are caught.

Then, too, there are seasons when game and animals move away from certain regions, and then the trapper cannot get them. Perhaps they go farther inland, and too far for him to follow. I have seen times when ptarmigans were so thick men killed them for dog food, and perhaps the next year there would not be a ptarmigan to be found to put into the pot for dinner. I have seen the snow trampled down everywhere in the woods and among the brush by innumerable snowshoe rabbits, and I have seen other years when not a single rabbit track was to be found anywhere. It is the same with caribou and the fur bearing animals as well. In those years when game is scarce the people are hard put to it to get a bit of fresh meat to eat.

When no fresh meat is to be had salt fish, bread (rarely with butter) and tea, with molasses as sweetening, is the diet. There is no milk, even for the babies. If all the salt fish has been sold or traded in for flour and tea, bread and tea three times a day is all there is to eat.

People cannot keep well on just bread and tea, or even bread and salt fish and tea. It is not hard for us to imagine how we would feel if every meal we had day in and day out was only bread and tea, and sometimes not enough of that.

X
THE SEAL HUNTER

No less perilous is the business of fisherman and sealer than that of hunter and trapper. Every turn a man makes down on The Labrador is likely to carry him into some adventure that will place his life in danger, at sea as on land. But there is no way out of it if a living is to be made.

It is a strange fact that one never recognizes a great deal of danger in the life that one is accustomed to living, no matter how perilous it may seem to others. If a Labradorman were to come to any of our towns or cities his heart would be in his mouth at every turn, for a time at least, dodging automobiles and street cars. It would appear to him an exceedingly hazardous existence that we live, and he would long to be back to the peace and quiet and safety of his sea and wilderness. And our streets would be dangerous ground to him, indeed, until he became accustomed to dodging motor cars. He is nimble enough, and on his own ground could put most of us to shame in that respect, but here he is lacking in experience.

The same hunter will face the storms and solitude of the wilderness trail without ever once feeling that he is in danger or afraid. He knows how to do it. That is the life that he has been reared to live. The average city man would perish in a day if left alone to care for himself on a trapper's trail. He has never learned the business, and he would not know how to take care of himself.

The Labradorman being both hunter and fisherman, is perfectly at home both in the wilderness and on the sea. He has the dangers of both to meet, but he does not recognize them as dangerous callings, though every year some mate or neighbor loses his life. "'Tis the way o' th' Lard."

Ice still covers the Labrador harbors in May, and this is when the seal hunt begins, or, as the liveyere says, he goes "swileing." He calls a seal a "swile." With a harpoon attached to a long line he stations himself at a breathing hole in the ice which the seals under the ice have kept open, and out of which, now and again, one raises its nose and fills its lungs with air, for seals are animals, not fish, and must have air to breathe or they will drown. The hole is a small one, but large enough to cast the spear, or harpoon, into.

Seals are exceedingly shy animals, and the slightest movement will frighten them away. Therefore the seal hunter must stand perfectly still, like a graven image, with harpoon poised, and that is pretty cold work in zero weather. If luck is with him he will after a time see a small movement in the water, and a moment later a seal's nose will appear. Then like a flash of lightning, he casts the harpoon, and if his aim is good, as it usually is, a seal is fast on the barbs of the harpoon.

The harpoon point is attached to a long line, while the harpoon shaft, by an ingenious arrangement, will slip free from the point. Now, while the shaft remains in the hands of the hunter, the line begins running rapidly down through the hole, for the seal in a vain endeavor to free itself dives deeply. The other end of the line also remaining in the hands of the hunter is fastened to the shaft of the harpoon, and there is a struggle. In time, the seal, unable to return to its hole for air, is drowned, and then is hauled out through the hole upon the ice.

These north Atlantic seals, having no fine fur like the Pacific seals, are chiefly valuable for their fat. The pelts are, however, of considerable value to the natives. The women tan them and make them into watertight boots or other clothing. Of course a good many of them find their way to civilization, where they are made into pocketbooks and bags, and they make a very fine tough leather indeed. The flesh is utilized for dog food, though, as in the case of young seals particularly, it is often eaten by the people, particularly when other sorts of meat is scarce. Most of the people, and particularly the Eskimos, are fond of the flippers and liver.

Sometimes the seals come out of their holes to lie on the ice and bask in the sun. Then the hunter, simulating the movements of a seal, crawls toward his game until he is within rifle shot.

Should a gale of wind arise suddenly, the ice may be separated into pans and drift abroad before the seal hunters can make their escape to land. In that case a hunter may be driven to sea on an ice pan, and he is fortunate if his neighbors discover him and rescue him in boats.

After the ice goes out, those who own seal nets set them, and a great many seals are caught in this way. At this season the seals frequently are seen sunning themselves on the shore rocks, and the hunters stalk and shoot them.

Newfoundlanders carry on their sealing in steamers built for the purpose. They go out to the great ice floe, far out to sea and quite too far for the liveyeres to reach in small craft. Here the seals are found in thousands. These vessels, depending upon the size, bring home a cargo sometimes numbering as many as 20,000 to 30,000 seals in a single ship, and there are about twenty-five ships in the fleet.

This terrible slaughter has seriously decreased the numbers. The Labrador Eskimos used to depend upon them largely for their living. They can do this no longer, for not every season, as formerly, are there enough seals to supply needs. All of the five varieties of North Atlantic seals are caught on the coast —harbor, jar, harp, hooded and square flipper. The last named is also called the great bearded seal and sometimes the sealion. The first named is the smallest of all.

Scarce a year passes that we do not hear of a serious disaster in the Newfoundland sealing fleet. Sometimes severe snow storms arise when the men are hunting on the floe, and then the men are often lost. Sometimes the ships are crushed in the big floe and go to the bottom. The latest of these disasters was the disappearance of the Southern Cross, with a crew of one hundred seventy-five men.

One of my good friends, Captain Jacob Kean, used to command the Virginia Lake, one of the largest of the sealers. She carried a crew of about two hundred men. A few years before Captain Kean lost his life in one of the awful sea disasters of the coast, he related to me one of his experiences at the sealing.

Captain Kean was in luck that year, and found the seals early and in great numbers. The crew had made a good hunt on the floe, and they are loading them with about a third of a cargo aboard when suddenly the ice closed in and the Virginia Lake was "pinched," with the result that a good sized hole was broken in her planking on the port side forward below the water line. The sea rushed in, and it looked for a time as though the vessel would sink, and there were not boats enough to accommodate the crew even if boats could have been used, which was hardly possible under the conditions, for the sea was clogged with heaving ice pans.

The pumps were manned, and Captain Kean, and with every man not working the pumps, with feverish haste shifted the cargo to the starboard side and aft. Presently, with the weight shifted, the ship lay over on her starboard side and her bow rose above the water until the crushed planking and the hole were above the water line.

The hole now exposed, Captain Kean stuffed it with sea biscuit, or hardtack. Over this he nailed a covering of canvas. Tubs of butter were brought up, and the canvas thoroughly and thickly buttered. This done, a sheathing of planking was spiked on over the buttered canvas. Then the cargo was re-shifted into place, the vessel settled back upon an even keel, and it was found that the leak was healed. The sea biscuit, absorbing moisture, swelled, and this together with the canvas, butter and planking proved effectual. Captain Kean loaded his ship with seals and took her into St. John's harbor safely with a full cargo.

The following year the Virginia Lake was again pinched by the ice, but this time was lost. Captain Kean and his crew took refuge on the ice floe, and were fortunately rescued by another sealer. When Captain Kean lost his life a few years later the sealing fleet lost one of its most successful masters. He was a fine Christian gentleman and as able a seaman as ever trod a bridge.

But this is the life of the sealer and the fisherman of the northern sees. Terrible storms sometimes sweep down that rugged, barren coast and leave behind them a harvest of wrecked vessels and drowned men and destitute families that have lost their only support.

These were the conditions that Grenfell found in Labrador, and this was the breed of men, these hunters and trappers, fishermen and sealers—sturdy, honest, God-fearing folk—with whom Grenfell took up his life. He had elected to share with them the hardships of their desolate land and the perils of their ice-choked sea. They needed him, and to them he offered a service that was Christ-like in its breadth and devotion.

It was a peculiar field. No ordinary man could have entered it with hope of success. Mere ability as a physician and surgeon of wide experience was not enough. In addition to this, success demanded that he be a Christian gentleman with high ideals, and freedom from bigotry. Courage, moral as well as physical, was a necessity. Only a man who was himself a fearless and capable navigator could make the rounds of the coast and respond promptly to the hurried and urgent calls to widely separated patients. Constant exposure to hardship and peril demanded a strong body and a level head. Balanced judgment, high executive and administrative ability, deep insight into human character and unbounded sympathy for those who suffered or were in trouble were indispensable characteristics. All of these attributes Grenfell possessed.

A short time before Mr. Moody's death, Grenfell met Moody and told him of the inspiration he had received from that sermon, delivered in London many years before by the great evangelist.

"What have you been doing since?" asked Moody.

What has Grenfell been doing since? He has established hospitals at Battle Harbor, Indian Harbor, Harrington and Northwest River in Labrador, and at St. Anthony in northeastern Newfoundland. He has established schools and nursing stations both in Labrador and Newfoundland. He has built and maintains two orphanages. He founded the Seamen's Institute in St. Johns.

Year after year, since that summer's day when the Albert anchored in Domino Run and Grenfell first met the men of the Newfoundland fishing fleet and the liveyeres of the Labrador coast, winter and summer, Grenfell himself and the doctors that assist him have patrolled that long desolate coast giving the best that was in them to the people that lived there. Grenfell has preached the Word, fed the hungry, clothed the naked, sheltered the homeless and righted many wrongs. He has fought disease and poverty, evil and oppression. Hardship, peril and prejudice have fallen to his lot, but he has met them with a courage and determination that never faltered, and he is still "up and at it."

Grenfell's life has been a life of service to others. Freely and joyfully he has given himself and all that was in him to the work of making others happier, and the people of the coast love and trust him. With pathetic confidence they lean upon him and call him in their need, as children lean upon their father, and he has never failed to respond. When a man who had lost a leg felt the need for an artificial one, he appealed to Grenfell:

Docter plase I whant to see you. Docter sir have you got a leg if you have Will you plase send him Down Praps he may fet and you would oblig.

One who wished clothing for his family wrote:

To Dr. Gransfield

Dear honrabel Sir,

I would be pleased to ask you Sir if you would be pleased to give me and my wife a littel poor close. I was going in the Bay to cut some wood. But I am all amost blind and cant Do much so if you would spear me some Sir I would Be very thankful to you Sir.

Calls to visit the sick are continuously received. The following are genuine examples:

Reverance dr. Grandfell. Dear sir we are expecting you hup and we would like for you to come so quick as you can for my dater is very sick with a very large sore under her left harm we emenangin that the old is two enchis deep and two enches wide plase com as quick as you can to save life I remains yours truely.

Docker—Please wel you send me somting for the pain in my feet and what you proismed to send my little boy. Docker I am almost cripple, it is up my hips, I can hardly walk. This is my housban is gaining you this note.

doctor—i have a compleant i ham weak with wind on the chest, weakness all over me up in my harm.

Dear Dr. Grenfell.

I would like for you to Have time to come Down to my House Before you leaves to go to St. Anthony. My little Girl is very Bad. it seems all in Her neck. Cant Ply her Neck forward if do she nearly goes in the fits. i dont know what it is the matter with Her myself. But if you would see Her you would know what the matter with Her. Please send a word by the Bearer what gives you this note and let me know where you will have time to come down to my House, i lives down the Bay a Place called Berry Head.

These people are made of the same clay as you and I. They are moved by the same human emotions. They love those who are near and dear to them no less than we love those who are near and dear to us. The same heights or depths of joy and sorrow, hopes and disappointments enter into their lives. In the following chapters let us meet some of them, and travel with Doctor Grenfell as he goes about his work among them.

XI
UNCLE WILLIE WOLFREY

One bitterly cold day in winter our dog team halted before a cabin. We had been hailed as we were passing by the man of the house. He gave us a hearty hand shake and invitation to have "a drop o' tea and a bit to eat," adding, "you'd never ha' been passin' without stoppin' for a cup o' tea to warm you up, whatever." It was early, and we had intended to stop farther on to boil our kettle in the edge of the woods with as little loss of time as possible, but there was no getting away from the hospitality of the liveyere.

There were three of us, and we were as hungry as bears, for there is nothing like snowshoe traveling in thirty and forty degrees below zero weather to give one an appetite. As we entered we sniffed a delicious odor of roasting meat, and that one sniff made us glad we had stopped, and made us equally certain we had never before in our lives been so hungry for a good meal. For days we had been subsisting on hardtack and jerked venison, two articles of food that will not freeze for they contain no moisture, and tea; or, when we stopped at a cabin, on bread and tea. The man's wife was already placing plates, cups and saucers on the bare table for us, and two little boys were helping with hungry eagerness.

"Hang your adikeys on the pegs there and get warmed up," our host invited. "Dinner's a'most ready. 'Tis a wonderful frosty day to be cruisin'."

We did as he directed, and then seated ourselves on chests that he pulled forward for seats. He had many questions to ask concerning the folk to the northward, their health and their luck at the winter's trapping, until, presently, the woman brought forth from the oven and placed upon the table a pan of deliciously browned, smoking meat.

"Set in! Set in!" beamed our host. "'Tis fine you comes today and not yesterday," adding as we drew up to the table: "All we'd been havin' to give you yesterday and all th' winter, were bread and tea. Game's been wonderful scarce, and this is the first bit o' meat we has th' whole winter, barrin' a pa'tridge or two in November. But this marnin' I finds a lynx in one o' my traps, and a fine prime skin he has. I'll show un to you after we eats, though he's on the dryin' board and you can't see the fur of he."

We bowed our heads while the host asked the blessing. The Labradorman rarely omits the blessing, and often the meal is closed with a final thanks, for men of the wilderness live near to God. He is very near to them and they reverence Him.

"Help yourself, sir! Help yourself!"

Each of us helped himself sparingly to the cat meat. There was bread, but no butter, and there was hot tea with black molasses for sweetening.

"Take more o' th' meat now! Help yourselves! Don't be afraid of un," our hospitable host urged, and we did help ourselves again, for it was good.

Whenever we passed within hailing distance of a cabin, we had to stop for a "cup o' hot tea, whatever." Otherwise the people would have felt sorely hurt. We seldom found more elaborate meals than bread, tea and molasses, rarely butter, and of course never any vegetables.

We soon discovered that we could not pay the head of the family for our entertainment, but where there were children we left money with the mother with which to buy something for the little ones, which doubtless would be clothing or provisions for the family. If there were no children we left the money on the table or somewhere where it surely would be discovered after our departure.

I remember one of this fine breed of men well. I met him on this journey, and he once drove dog team for me—Uncle Willie Wolfrey. Doctor Grenfell says of him:

"Uncle Willie isn't a scholar, a social light, or a capitalist magnate, but all the same ten minutes' visit to Uncle Willie Wolfrey is worth five dollars of any man's investment."

It requires a lot of physical energy for any man to tramp the trails day after day through a frigid, snow-covered wilderness, and months of it at a stretch. It is a big job for a young and hearty man, and a tremendous one for a man of Uncle Willie's years. And it is a man's job, too, to handle a boat in all weather, in calm and in gale, in clear and in fog, sixteen to twenty hours a day, and the fisherman's day is seldom shorter than that. The fish must be caught when they are there to be caught, and they must be split and salted the day they are caught, and then there's the work of spreading them on the "flakes," and turning them, and piling and covering them when rain threatens.

A cataract began to form on Uncle Willie's eyes, and every day he could see just a little less plainly than the day before. The prospects were that he would soon be blind, and without his eyesight he could neither hunt nor fish.

But with his growing age and misfortune Uncle Willie was never a whit less cheerful. He had to earn his living and he kept at his work.

"'Tis the way of the Lard," said he. "He's blessed me with fine health all my life, and kept the house warm, and we've always had a bit to eat, whatever. The Lard has been wonderful good to us, and I'll never be complainin'."

It was never Uncle Willie's way to complain about hard luck. He always did his best, and somehow, no matter how hard a pinch in which he found himself, it always came out right in the end.

Finally Uncle Willie's eyesight became so poor that it was difficult for him to see sufficiently to get around, and one day last summer (1921) he stepped off his fish stage where he was at work, and the fall broke his thigh. This happened at the very beginning of the fishing season, and put an end to the summer's fishing for Uncle Willie, and, of course, to all hope of hunting and trapping during last winter.

Then Doctor Grenfell happened along with his brave old hospital ship Strathcona. Dr. Grenfell has a way of happening along just when people are desperately in need of him. With Dr. Grenfell was Dr. Morlan, a skillful and well-known eye and throat specialist from Chicago. Dr. Morlan was spending his holiday with Dr. Grenfell, helping heal the sick down on The Labrador, giving free his services and his great skill.

Dr. Grenfell set and dressed Uncle Willie Wolfrey's broken thigh. Dr. Morlan was to remain but a few days. If he were to help Uncle Willie's eyes there could be no time given for a recovery from the operation on the thigh. Uncle Willie was game for it.

They had settled Uncle Willie comfortably at Indian Harbor Hospital, and immediately the thigh was set Dr. Morlan operated upon one of the eyes. The operation was successful, and when the freeze-up came with the beginning of winter, Uncle Willie, hobbling about on crutches and with one good eye was home again in his cabin.

Uncle Willie lives in a lonely place, and for many miles north and south he has but one neighbor. The outlook for the winter was dismal indeed. His flour barrel was empty. He had no money.

But that stout old heart could not be discouraged or subdued. Uncle Willie was as full of grit as ever he was in his life. He was still a fountain of cheery optimism and hope. He could see with one eye now, and out of that eye the world looked like a pretty good place in which to live, and he was decided to make the best of it.

Dr. Grenfell, passing down the coast, called in to see the crippled old fisherman and hunter, and in commenting on that visit he said:

"There are certain men it always does one good to meet. Uncle Willie is a channel of blessing. His sincerity and faith do one good. There is always a merry glint in his eye. Even with one eye out, and his crutches on, and his prospect of hunger, Uncle Willie was just the same."

Dr. Grenfell left some money, donated by the Doctor's friends, and made other provisions for the comfort of Uncle Willie Wolfrey during the winter. If all goes well he will be at his fishing again, when the ice clears away; and the snows of another winter will see him again on his trapping path setting traps for martens and foxes. And with his rifle and one good eye, who knows but he may knock over a silver fox or a bear or two?

Good luck to Uncle Willie Wolfrey and his spirit, which cannot be downed.

As Dr. Grenfell has often said, the Labradorman is a fountain of faith and hope and inspiration. If the fishing season is a failure he turns to his winter's trapping with unwavering faith that it will yield him well. If his trapping fails his hope and faith are none the less when he sets out in the spring to hunt seals. Seals may be scarce and the reward poor, but never mind! The summer fishing is at hand, andthis year it will certainly bring a good catch! "The Lard be wonderful good to us, whatever."

XII
A DOZEN FOX TRAPS

On that same voyage along the coast when Uncle Willie Wolfrey was found with a broken thigh, Dr. Grenfell, after he had operated upon Uncle Willie, in the course of his voyage, stopping at many harbors to give medical assistance to the needy ones, ran in one day to Kaipokok Bay, at Turnavik Islands.

As the vessel dropped her anchor he observed a man sitting on the rocks eagerly watching the ship. The jolly boat was launched, and as it approached the land the man arose and coming down to the water's edge, shouted:

"Be that you, Doctor?"

"Yes, Uncle Tom, it is I?" the Doctor shouted back, for he had already recognized Uncle Tom, one of the fine old men of the coast.

When Grenfell stepped ashore and took Uncle Tom's hand in a hearty grasp, the old man broke down and cried like a child. Uncle Tom was evidently in keen distress.

"Oh, Doctor, I'm so glad you comes. I were lookin' for you, Doctor," said the old man in a voice broken by emotion. "I were watchin' and watchin' out here on the rocks, not knowin' whether you'd be comin' this way, but hopin', and prayin' the Lard to send you. He sends you, Doctor. 'Twere the Lard sends you when I'm needin' you, sir, sorely needin' you."

Uncle Tom is seventy years of age. He was born and bred on The Labrador, but he has not spent all his life there. In his younger days he shipped as a sailor, and as a seaman saw many parts of the world. But long ago he returned to his home to settle down as a fisherman and a trapper.

When the war came, the brave old soul, stirred by patriotism, paid his own passage and expenses on the mail boat to St. Johns, and offered to volunteer for service. Of course he was too old and was rejected because of his age.

Uncle Tom, his patriotism not in the least dampened, returned to his Labrador home and divided all the fur of his winter's hunt into two equal piles. To one pile he added a ten dollar bill, and that pile, with the ten dollars added, he shipped at once to the "Patriotic Fund" in St. Johns. He had offered himself, and they would not take him, and this was all he could do to help win the war, and he did it freely and wistfully, out of his noble, generous patriotic soul.

"What is the trouble, Uncle Tom?" asked Grenfell, when Uncle Tom had to some extent regained his composure, and the old man told his story.

He was in hard luck. Late the previous fall (1920) or early in the winter he had met with a severe accident that had resulted in several broken ribs. Navigation had closed, and he was cut off from all surgical assistance, and his broken ribs had never had attention and had not healed. He could scarcely draw a breath without pain, or even rest without pain at night, and he could not go to his trapping path.

He depended upon his winter's hunt mainly for support, and with no fur to sell he was, for the first time in his life, compelled to contract a debt. Then, suddenly, the trader with whom he dealt discontinued giving credit. Uncle Tom was stranded high and dry, and when the fishing season came he had no outfit or means of purchasing one, and could not go fishing.

Besides his wife there were six children in Uncle Tom's family, though none of them was his own or related to him. When the "flu" came to the coast in 1918, and one out of every five of the people around Turnavik Islands died, several little ones were left homeless and orphans. The generous hearts of Uncle Tom and his wife opened to them and they took these six children into their home as their own. And so it happened that Uncle Tom had, and still has, a large family depending upon him.

"As we neared the cottage," said Doctor Grenfell, "his good wife, beaming from head to foot as usual, came out to greet us. Optimist to the last ditch, she knew that somehow provision would be made. She, too, had had her troubles, for twice she had been operated on at Indian Harbor for cancer."

Uncle Tom must have suffered severely during all those months that he had lived with his broken ribs uncared for. Now Dr. Grenfell, without loss of time, strapped them up good and tight. Mrs. Grenfell supplied the six youngsters with a fine outfit of good warm clothes, and when Dr. Grenfell sailed out of Kaipokok Bay Uncle Tom and Mrs. Tom had no further cause for worry concerning the source from which provisions would come for themselves and the six orphans they had adopted.

These are but a few incidents in the life of the people to whom Dr. Grenfell is devoting his skill and his sympathy year in and year out. I could relate enough of them to fill a dozen volumes like this, but space is limited.

There is always hardship and always will be in a frontier land like Labrador, and Labrador north of Cape Charles is the most primitive of frontier lands. Dr. Grenfell and his helpers find plenty to do in addition to giving out medicines and dressing wounds. A little boost sometimes puts a family on its feet, raising it from abject poverty to independence and self-respect. Just a little momentum to push them over the line. Grenfell knows how to do this.

Several years ago Dr. Grenfell anchored his vessel in Big Bight, and went ashore to visit David Long. David had had a hard winter, and among other kindnesses to the family, Dr. Grenfell presented David's two oldest boys, lads of fifteen or sixteen or thereabouts, with a dozen steel fox traps. Lack of traps had prevented the boys taking part in trapping during the previous winter.

The next year after giving the boys the traps, Grenfell again cast anchor in Big Bight, and, as usual, rowed ashore to visit the Longs. There was great excitement in their joyous greeting. Something important had happened. There was no doubt of that! David and Mrs. Long and the two lads and all the little Longs were exuding mystery, but particularly the two lads. Whatever this mysterious secret was they could scarce keep it until they had led Dr. Grenfell into the cabin, and he was comfortably seated.

Then, with vast importance and some show of deliberate dignity, David opened a chest. From its depths he drew forth a pelt. Dr. Grenfell watched with interest while David shook it to make the fur stand out to best advantage, and then held up to his admiring gaze the skin of a beautiful silver fox! The lads had caught it in one of the dozen traps he had given them.

"We keeps un for you," announced David exultantly.

"It's a prime one, too!" exclaimed the Doctor, duly impressed, as he examined it.

"She be that," emphasized David proudly. "No finer were caught on the coast the winter."

"It was a good winter's work," said the Doctor.

"'Twere that now! 'Twere a wonderful good winter's work—just t'cotch that un!" enthused Mrs. Long.

"What are you going to do with it?" asked Doctor Grenfell.

"We keeps un for you," said David. "The time was th' winter when we has ne'er a bit o' grub but what we hunts, all of our flour and molasses gone. But we don't take he to the trade, whatever. We keeps he for you."

Out on a coast island Captain William Bartlett, of Brigus, Newfoundland, kept a fishing station and a supply store. Captain Will is a famous Arctic navigator. He is one of the best known and most successful masters of the great sealing fleet. He is also a cod fisherman of renown and he is the father of Captain

"Bob" Bartlett, master of explorer Peary's Roosevelt, and it was under Captain Will Bartlett's instruction that Captain "Bob" learned seamanship and navigation. Captain William Bartlett is as fine a man as ever trod a deck. He is just and honest to a degree, and he has a big generous heart.

Doctor Grenfell accepted the silver fox pelt, and as he steamed down the coast he ran his vessel in at Captain Bartlett's station. He had confidence in Captain Bartlett.

"Here's a silver fox skin that belongs to David Long's lads," said he, depositing the pelt on the counter. "I wish you'd take it, and do the best you can for David, Captain Will. I'll leave it with you."

Captain Bartlett shook the pelt out, and admired its lustrous beauty.

"It's a good one! David's lads were in luck when they caught that fellow. I'll do the best I can with it," he promised.

"They'll take the pay in provisions and other necessaries," suggested Grenfell.

"All right," agreed Captain Will. "I'll send the goods over to them."

On his way to the southward a month later Doctor Grenfell again cast anchor at Big Bight. David Long and Mrs. Long, the two big lads, and all the little Longs, were as beaming and happy as any family could be in the whole wide world. Captain Bartlett's vessel had run in at Big Bight one day, and paid for the silver fox pelt in merchandise.

The cabin was literally packed with provisions. The family were well clothed. There was enough and to spare to keep them in affluence, as affluence goes down on The Labrador, for a whole year and longer. Need and poverty were vanished. Captain Will had, indeed, done well with the silver fox pelt.

These are stories of life on The Labrador as Doctor Grenfell found it. From the day he reached the coast and every day since his heart has ached with the troubles and poverty existing among the liveyeres. He has been thrilled again and again by incidents of heroic struggle and sacrifice among them. He has done a vast deal to make them more comfortable and happy, as in the case of David Long. Still, in spite of it all, there are cases of desperate poverty and suffering there, and doubtless will always be.

In every city and town and village of our great and prosperous country people throw away clothing and many things that would help to make the lives of the Longs and the hundreds of other liveyeres of the coast who are toiling for bare existence easier to endure. Enough is wasted every year, indeed, in any one of our cities to make the whole population of Labrador happy and comfortable. And there's the pity. If Grenfell could only be given some of this waste to take to them!

From the beginning this thought troubled Doctor Grenfell. And in winter when the ice shuts the whole coast off from the rest of the world, he turned his attention to efforts to secure the help of good people the world over in his work. Making others happy is the greatest happiness that any one can experience, and Grenfell wished others to share his happiness with him. Nearly every winter for many years he has lectured in the United States and Canada and Great Britain with this in view. The Grenfell Association was organized with headquarters in New York, where money and donations of clothing and other necessaries might be sent.

As we shall see, many great things have been accomplished by Doctor Grenfell and this Association, organized by his friends several years ago. Every year a great many boxes and barrels of clothing go to him down on The Labrador, filled with good things for the needy ones. Boys and girls, as well as men and women, send warm things for winter. Not only clothing, but now and again toys for the Wee Tots find their way into the boxes. Just like other children the world over, the Wee Tots of The Labrador like toys to play with and they are made joyous with toys discarded by the over-supplied youngsters of our land.

Of course there are foolish people who send useless things too. Scattered through the boxes are now and again found evening clothes for men and women, silk top hats, flimsy little women's bonnets, dancing pumps, and even crepe-de-chene nighties. These serve as playthings for the grown-ups, many of whom, especially the Indians and Eskimos, are quite childlike with gimcracks. I recall once seeing an Eskimo parading around on a warm day in the glory of a full dress coat and silk hat, the coat drawn on over his ordinary clothing. He was the envy of his friends.

While Grenfell dispensed medical and surgical treatment, and at the same time did what he could for the needy, he also turned his attention to an attack upon the truck system. This system of barter was responsible for the depths of poverty in which he found the liveyeres. He was mightily wrought up against it, as well he might have been, and still is, and he laid plans at once to relieve the liveyeres and northern Newfoundlanders from its grip.

This was a great undertaking. It was a stroke for freedom, for the truck system, as we have seen, is simply a species of slavery. He realized that in attacking it he was to create powerful enemies who would do their utmost to injure him and interfere with his work. Some of these men he knew would go to any length to drive him off The Labrador. It required courage, but Grenfell was never lacking in courage. He rolled up his sleeves and went at it. He always did things openly and fearlessly, first satisfying himself he was right.

SKIPPER TOM'S COD TRAP

Skipper Tom lived, and for aught I know still lives, at Red Bay, a little settlement on the Straits of Belle Isle, some sixty miles to the westward of Battle Harbor.

Along the southern coast of Labrador the cabins are much closer together than on the east coast, and there are some small settlements in the bays and harbors, with snug little painted cottages.

Red Bay, where Skipper Tom lived, is one of these settlements. It boasts a neat little Methodist chapel, built by the fishermen and trappers from lumber cut in the near-by forest, and laboriously sawn into boards with the pit saw.

Skipper Tom lived in one of the snuggest and coziest of the cottages. I remember the cottage and I remember Skipper Tom well. I happened into the settlement one evening directly ahead of a winter blizzard, and Skipper Tom and his good family opened their little home to me and sheltered me with a hospitable cordial welcome for three days, until the weather cleared and the dogs could travel again and I pushed forward on my journey.

Skipper Tom stood an inch or two above six feet in his moccasins. He was a broad-shouldered, strong-limbed man of the wilderness and the sea. His face was kindly and gentle, but at the same time reflected firmness, strength and thoughtfulness. When he spoke you were sure to listen, for there was always the conviction that he was about to utter some word of wisdom, or tell you something of importance. The moment you looked at him and heard his voice you said to yourself: "Here is a man upon whom I can rely and in whom I can place absolute confidence."

If Skipper Tom promised to do anything, he did it, unless Providence intervened. If he said he would not do a thing, he would not do it, and you could depend on it. He was a man of his word. That was Skipper Tom—big, straight spoken, and as square as any man that ever lived. That is what his neighbors said of him, and that is the way Doctor Grenfell found him.

Now and again the Methodist missionary visited Red Bay in his circuit of the settlements, and when he came he made his headquarters in the home of Skipper Tom. On the occasion of these visits he conducted services in the chapel on Sunday, and on week days visited every home in Red Bay. Skipper Tom was class leader, and looked after the religious welfare of the little community, presiding over his class in the chapel, on the great majority of Sundays, when the missionary was engaged elsewhere.

The people looked up to Skipper Tom. The folk of Red Bay, like most people who live much in the open and close to nature, have a deep religious reverence and a wholesome fear of God. As their class leader Skipper Tom guided them in their worship, and they looked upon him as an example of upright living. So it was that he had a great burden of responsibility, with the morals of the community thrust upon him.

In one respect Skipper Tom was fortunate. He did not inherit a debt, and all his life he had kept free from the truck system under which his neighbors toiled hopelessly, year in and year out.

He had, in one way or another, picked up enough education to read and write and figure. He could read and interpret his Bible and he could calculate his accounts. He knew that two times two make four. If he sold two hundred quintals of fish at $2.25 a quintal, he knew that $450.00 were due him. No trader had a mortgage upon the product of his labor, as they had upon that of his neighbors, and he was free to sell his fur and fish to whoever would pay him the highest price.

To be sure there were seasons when Skipper Tom was hard put to it to make ends meet, and a scant diet and a good many hardships fell to his lot and to the lot of his family. And when he had enough and his neighbors were in need, he denied himself to see others through, and even pinched himself to do it.

But he saved bit by bit until, at the age of forty-five, he was able to purchase a cod trap, which was valued at about $400.00. The purchase of this cod trap had been the ambition of his life and we can imagine his joy when finally the day came that brought it to him. It made more certain his catch of cod, and therefore lessened the possibility of winters of privation.

It is interesting to know how the fishermen of The Labrador catch cod. It may be worth while also to explain that when the Labradorman or Newfoundlander speaks of "fish" he means cod in his vocabulary. A trout is a trout, a salmon is a salmon and a caplin is a caplin, but a cod is a fish. He never thinks of anything as fish but cod.

Early in the season, directly the ice breaks up, a little fish called the caplin, which is about the size of a smelt, runs inshore in great schools of countless millions, to spawn. I have seen them lying in windrows along the shore where the receding tide had left them high and dry upon the land. This is a great time for the dogs, which feast upon them and grow fat. It is a great time also for the cod, which feed on the caplin, and for the fishermen who catch the cod. Cod follow the caplin schools, and this is the season when the fisherman, if he is so fortunate as to own a trap, reaps his greatest harvest.

The trap is a net with four sides and a bottom, but no top. It is like a great room without a ceiling. On one side is a door or opening. The trap is submerged a hundred yards or so from shore, at a point where the caplin, with the cod at their heels, are likely to run in. A net attached to the trap at the center of the door is stretched to the nearest shore.

Like a flock of geese that follows the old gander cod follow their leaders. When the leaders pilot the school in close to shore in pursuit of the caplin, they encounter the obstructing net, then follow along its side with the purpose of going around it. This leads them into the trap. Once into the trap they remain there until the fishermen haul their catch.

The fisherman who owns no trap must rely upon the hook and line. Though sometimes hook and line fishermen meet with good fortune, the results are much less certain than with the traps and the work much slower and vastly more difficult.

When the water is not too deep jigging with unbaited hooks proves successful when fish are plentiful. Two large hooks fastened back to back, with lead to act as a sinker, serve the purpose. This double hook at the end of the line is dropped over the side of the boat and lowered until it touches bottom. Then it is raised about three feet, and from this point "jigged," or raised and lowered continuously until taken by a cod.

In deep water, however, bait is necessary and the squid is a favorite bait. A squid is a baby octopus, or "devil fish." The squid is caught by jigging up and down a lead weight filled with wire spikes and painted bright red. It seizes the weight with its tentacles. When raised into the boat it releases its hold and squirts a small stream of black inky fluid. In the water, when attacked, this inky fluid discolors the water and screens it from its enemy.

The octopus grows to immense size, with many long arms. Two Newfoundlanders were once fishing in an open boat, when an octopus attacked the boat, reaching for it with two enormous arms, with the purpose of dragging it down. One of the fishermen seized an ax that lay handy in the boat and chopped the arms off. The octopus sank and all the sea about was made black with its screen of ink. The sections of arms cut off were nineteen feet in length. They are still on exhibition in the St. Johns Museum, where I have seen them many times. Shortly afterward a dead octopus was found, measuring, with tentacles spread, forty feet over all. It was not, however, the same octopus which attacked the fishermen, for that must have been much larger.

We can understand, then, how much Skipper Tom's cod trap meant to him. We can visualize his pleasure, and share his joy. The trap was, to a large extent, insurance against privation and hardship. It was his reward for the self-denial of himself and his family for years, and represented his life's savings.

When at last the ice cleared from his fishing place and the trap was set, there was no prouder or happier man on The Labrador than Skipper Tom. The trap was in the water when the Princess May, one Saturday afternoon, steamed into Red Bay and Doctor Grenfell accepted the hospitable invitation of Skipper

Tom to spend the night at his home.

It was still early in the season and icebergs were plentiful enough, as, indeed, they are the whole summer long. They are always a menace to cod traps, for should a berg drift against a trap, that will be the end of the trap forever. Fishermen watch their traps closely, and if an iceberg comes so near as to threaten it the trap must be removed to save it. A little lack of watchfulness leads to ruin.

"The trap's well set," said Skipper Tom, when Doctor Grenfell inquired concerning it. "The ice is keepin' clear, but I watches close."

"What are the signs of fish?" asked the Doctor.

"Fine!" said Skipper Tom. "The signs be wonderful fine."

"I hope you'll have a big year."

"There's a promise of un," Skipper Tom grinned happily. "The trap's sure to do fine for us."

But nobody knows from one day to another what will happen on The Labrador.

According to habit Skipper Tom was up bright and early on Sunday morning and went for a look at the trap. When presently he returned to join Doctor Grenfell at breakfast he was plainly worried.

"There's a berg driftin' down on the trap. We'll have to take her in," he announced.

"But 'tis Sunday," exclaimed his wife. "You'll never be workin' on Sunday."

"Aye, 'tis Sunday and 'tis against my principles to fish on the Sabbath day. I never did before, but 'tis to save our cod trap now. The lads and I'll not fish. We'll just haul the trap."

"The Lard'll forgive that, whatever," agreed his wife.

Skipper Tom went out when he had eaten, but it was not long until he returned.

"I'm not goin' to haul the trap today," he said quietly and decisively. "There are those in this harbor," he added, turning to Doctor Grenfell, "who would say, if I hauled that trap, that 'twould be no worse for them to fish on Sunday than for me to haul my trap. Then they'd go fishin' Sundays the same as other days, and none of un would keep Sunday any more as a day of rest, as the Lard intends us to keep un, and has told us in His own words we must keep un. I'll not haul the trap this day, though 'tis sore hard to lose un."

For a principle, and because he was well aware of his influence upon the folk of the settlement, Skipper Tom had made his decision to sacrifice his cod trap and the earnings of his lifetime. His conscience told him it would be wrong to do a thing that might lead others to do wrong. When our conscience tells us it is wrong to do a thing, it is wrong for us to do it. Conscience is the voice of God. If we disobey our conscience God will soon cease to speak to us through it. That is the way every criminal in the world began his downward career. He disobeyed his conscience, and continued to disobey it until he no longer heard it.

Skipper Tom never disobeyed his conscience. Now the temptation was strong. His whole life's savings were threatened to be swept away. There was still time to save the trap.

But Skipper Tom was strong. He turned his back upon the cod trap and the iceberg and temptation, and as he and Doctor Grenfell climbed the hill to the chapel he greeted his neighbors calmly and cheerily.

Every eye in Red Bay was on Skipper Tom that day. Every person knew of the cod trap and its danger, and all that it meant to Skipper Tom, and the temptation Skipper Tom was facing; but from all outward appearance he had dismissed the cod trap and the iceberg from his mind.

When dusk fell that night the iceberg was almost upon the cod trap.

XIV
THE SAVING OF RED BAY

At an early hour on Sunday evening Skipper Tom went to his bed as usual, and it is quite probable that within a period of ten minutes after his head rested upon his pillow he was sleeping peacefully. There was nothing else to do. He had no doubt that his cod trap was lying under the iceberg a hopeless wreck.

Well, what of it? In any case he had acted as his conscience had him act. He knew that there were those who would say that his conscience was oversensitive. Perhaps it was, but it was his conscience, not theirs. He was class leader in the chapel. He never forgot that. And he was the leading citizen of the settlement. At whatever cost, he must needs prove a good example to his neighbors in his deeds. Worry would not help the case in the least. Too much of it would incapacitate him. He had lived forty-four years without a cod trap, and he had not starved, and he could finish his days without one.

"The Lard'll take care of us," Skipper Tom often said when they were in a tight pinch, but he always added, "if we does our best to make the best of things and look after ourselves and the things the Lard gives us to do with. He calls on us to do that."

Though Skipper Tom could scarce see how his trap might have escaped destruction he had no intention of resting upon that supposition and perhaps he still entertained a lingering hope that it had escaped. There is no doubt he prayed for its preservation, and he had strong faith in prayer. At any rate, at half past eleven o'clock that night he was up and dressed, and routed his two sons out of their beds. At the stroke of midnight, waiting a tick longer perhaps, to be quite sure that Sunday had gone and Monday morning had arrived, he and his sons pushed out in their big boat.

Skipper Tom would not be doing his best if he did not make certain of what had actually happened to the cod trap. Every one in Red Bay said it had been destroyed, and no doubt of that. But no one knew for a certainty, and there might have been an intervention of Divine Providence.

"The Lard helped us to get that trap," said Skipper Tom, "and 'tis hard to believe he'll take un away from us so soon, for I tried not to be vain about un, only just a bit proud of un and glad I has un. If He's took un from me I'll know 'twere to try my faith, and I'll never complain."

Down they rowed toward the iceberg, whose polished surface gleamed white in the starlight.

"She's right over where the trap were set! The trap's gone," said one of the sons.

"I'm doubtin'," Skipper Tom was measuring the distance critically with his eye.

"The trap's tore to pieces," insisted the son with discouragement in his voice.

"The berg's to the lee'ard of she," declared Skipper Tom finally.

"Tis too close t' shore."

"'Tis to the lee'ard!"

"Is you sure, now, Pop?"

"The trap's safe and sound! The berg is t' the lee'ard!"

Tom was right. A shift of tide had come at the right moment to save the trap.

"The Lard is good to us," breathed Skipper Tom. "He've saved our trap! He always takes care of them that does what they feels is right. We'll thank the Lard, lads."

In the trap was a fine haul of cod, and when they had removed the fish the trap was transferred to a new position where it would be quite safe until the menacing iceberg had drifted away.

There were seventeen families living in Red Bay. As settlements go, down on The Labrador, seventeen cabins, each housing a family, is deemed a pretty good sized place.

At Red Bay, as elsewhere on the coast, bad seasons for fishing came now and again. These occur when the ice holds inshore so long that the best run of cod has passed before the men can get at them; or because for some unexplained reason the cod do not appear at all along certain sections of the coast. When two bad seasons come in succession, starvation looms on the horizon.

Seasons when the ice held in, Skipper Tom could not set his cod trap. When this happened he was as badly off as any of his neighbors. In a season when there were no fish to catch, it goes without saying that his trap brought him no harvest. Fishing and trapping is a gamble at best, and Skipper Tom, like his neighbors, had to take his chance, and sometimes lost. If he accumulated anything in the good seasons, he used his accumulation to assist the needy ones when the bad seasons came, and, in the end, though he kept out of debt, he could not get ahead, try as he would.

The seasons of 1904 and 1905 were both poor seasons, and when, in the fall of 1905, Doctor Grenfell's vessel anchored in Red Bay Harbor he found that several of the seventeen families had packed their belongings and were expectantly awaiting his arrival in the hope that he would take them to some place where they might find better opportunities. They were destitute and desperate.

There was nowhere to take them where their condition would be better. Grenfell, already aware of their desperate poverty, had been giving the problem much consideration. The truck system was directly responsible for the conditions at Red Bay and for similar conditions at every other harbor along the coast. Something had to be done, and done at once.

With the assistance of Skipper Tom and one or two others, Doctor Grenfell called a meeting of the people of the settlement that evening, to talk the matter over. The men and women were despondent and discouraged, but nearly all of them believed they could get on well enough if they could sell their fish and fur at a fair valuation, and could buy their supplies at reasonable prices.

All of them declared they could no longer subsist at Red Bay upon the restricted outfits allowed them by the traders, which amounted to little or nothing when the fishing failed. They preferred to go somewhere else and try their luck where perhaps the traders would be more liberal. If they remained at Red Bay under the old conditions they would all starve, and they might as well starve somewhere else.

Doctor Grenfell then suggested his plan. It was this. They would form a company. They would open a store for themselves. Through the store their furs and fish would be sent to market and they would get just as big a price for their products as the traders got. They would buy the store supplies at wholesale just as cheaply as the traders could buy them. They would elect one of their number, who could keep accounts, to be storekeeper. They would buy the things they needed from the store at a reasonable price, and at the end of the year each would be credited with his share of the profits. In other words, they would organize a co-operative store and trading system and be their own traders and storekeepers.

This meant breaking off from the traders with whom they had always dealt and all hope of ever securing advance of supplies from them again. It was a hazardous venture for the fishermen to make. They did not understand business, but they were desperate and ready for any chance that offered relief, and in the end they decided to do as Doctor Grenfell suggested.

Each man was to have a certain number of shares of stock in the new enterprise. The store would be supplied at once, and each family would be able to get from it what was needed to live upon during the winter. Any fish they might have on hand would be turned over to the store, credited as cash, and sent to market at once, in a schooner to be chartered for the purpose and this schooner would bring back to Red Bay the winter's supplies.

A canvass then was made with the result that among the seventeen families the entire assets available for purchasing supplies amounted to but eighty-five dollars. This was little better than nothing.

Doctor Grenfell had faith in Skipper Tom and the others. They were honest and hard-working folk. He knew that all they required was an opportunity to make good. He was determined to give them the opportunity, and he announced, without hesitation, that he would personally lend them enough to pay for the first cargo and establish the enterprise. Can any one wonder that the people love Grenfell? He was the one man in the whole world that would have done this, or who had the courage to do it. He knew well enough that he was calling down upon his own head the wrath of the traders.

The schooner was chartered, the store was stocked and opened, and there was enough to keep the people well-fed, well-clothed, happy and comfortable through the first year.

In the beginning there were some of the men who were actually afraid to have it known they were interested in the store, such was the fear with which the traders had ruled them. They were so timid, indeed, about the whole matter that they requested no sign designating the building as a store be placed upon it. That, they declared, would make the traders angry, and no one knew to what lengths these former slaveholders might go to have revenge upon them. It is no easy matter to shake oneself free from the traditions of generations and it was hard for these trappers and fishermen to realize that they were freed from their ancient bondage. But Doctor Grenfell fears no man, and, with his usual aggressiveness, he nailed upon the front of the store a big sign, reading:

RED BAY CO-OPERATIVE STORE.

It was during the winter of 1905-1906 and ten years after the launching of the enterprise and the opening of the store, that I drove into Red Bay with a train of dogs one cold afternoon. Skipper Tom was my host, and after we had a cheery cup of tea, he said:

"Come out. I wants to show you something."

He led me a little way down from his cottage to the store, and pointing up at the big bold sign, which Grenfell had nailed there, he announced proudly:

"'Tis our co-operative store, the first on the whole coast. Doctor Grenfell starts un for us."

Then after a pause:

"Doctor Grenfell be a wonderful man! He be a man of God."

As expected, there was a furore among the little traders when the news was spread that a co-operative store had been opened in Red Bay. The big Newfoundland traders and merchants were heartily in favor of it, and even stood ready to give the experiment their support.

But the little traders who had dealt with the Red Bay settlement for so long, and had bled the people and grown fat upon their labors, were bitterly hostile. They began a campaign of defamation against Doctor Grenfell and his whole field of work. They questioned his honesty, and criticised the conduct of his hospitals. They even enlisted the support of a Newfoundland paper in their opposition to him. They did everything in their power to drive him from the coast, so that they would have the field again in their own greedy hands. It was a dastardly exhibition of selfishness, but there are people in the world who will sell their own souls for profit.

Grenfell went on about his business of making people happier. He was in the right. If the traders would fight he would give it to them. He was never a quitter. He was the same Grenfell that beat up the big boy at school, years before. He was going to have his way about it, and do what he went to Labrador to do. He was going to do more. He was determined now to improve the trading conditions of the people of Labrador and northern Newfoundland, as well as to heal their sick.

From the day the co-operative store was opened in Red Bay not one fish and not one pelt of fur has ever gone to market from that harbor through a trader. The store has handled everything and it has prospered and the people have prospered beyond all expectation. Every one at Red Bay lives comfortably now. The debt to Doctor Grenfell was long since paid and cancelled. And it is characteristic of him that he would not accept one cent of interest. Shares of stock in the store, originally issued at five dollars a share, are now worth one hundred and four dollars a share, the difference being represented by profits that have not been withdrawn. Every share is owned by the people of the prosperous little settlement.

Up and down the Labrador coast and in northern Newfoundland nine co-operative stores have been established by Doctor Grenfell since that autumn evening when he met the Red Bay folk in conference and they voted to stake their all, even their life, in the venture that proved so successful. Two or three of the stores had to discontinue because the people in the localities where they were placed lived so far apart that there were not enough of them to make a store successful.

Every one of these stores was a great venture to the people who cast their lot with it. True they had little in money, but the stake of their venture was literally in each case their life. The man who never ventures never succeeds. Opportunity often comes to us in the form of a venture. Sometimes, it is a desperate venture too.

Doctor Grenfell had to fight the traders all along the line. They even had the Government of Newfoundland appoint a Commission to inquire into the operation of the Missions as a "menace to honest trade." A menace to honest trade! Think of it!

The result of the investigation proved that Grenfell and his mission was doing a big self-sacrificing work, and the finest kind of work to help the poor folk, and were doing it at a great cost and at no profit to the mission. So down went the traders in defeat.

The fellow that's right is the fellow that wins in the end. The fellow that's wrong is the fellow that is going to get the worst of it at the proper time. Grenfell only tried to help others. He never reaped a penny of personal gain. He always came out on top.

It's a good thing to be a scrapper sometimes, but if you're a scrapper be a good one. Grenfell is a scrapper when it is necessary, and when he has to scrap he goes at it with the best that's in him. He never does things half way. He never was a quitter. When he starts out to do anything he does it.

XV
A LAD OF THE NORTH

The needs of the children attracted Dr. Grenfell's attention from the beginning. A great many of them were neglected because the parents were too poor to provide for them properly. Those who were orphaned were thrown upon the care of their neighbors, and though the neighbors were willing they were usually too poor to take upon themselves this added burden.

There were no schools save those conducted by the Brethren of the Moravian missions among the Eskimos to the northward, and these were Eskimo schools where the people were taught to read and write in their own strange language, and to keep their accounts. But for the English speaking folk south of the Eskimo coast no provision for schools had ever been made.

The hospitals were overflowing with the sick or injured, and there was no room for children, unless they were in need of medical or surgical attention. There was great need of a home for the orphans where they would be cared for and receive motherly training and attention and could go to school.

Dr. Grenfell had thought about this a great deal. He had made the best arrangements possible for the actually destitute little ones by finding more or less comfortable homes for them, and seeking contributions from generous folk in the United States, Canada and Great Britain to pay for their expense.

But it was not, perhaps, until Pomiuk, a little Eskimo boy, came under his care that he finally decided that the establishment of a children's home could no longer be delayed.

Pomiuk's home was in the far north of Labrador, where no trees grow, and where the seasons are quite as frigid as those of northern Greenland. In summer he lived with his father and mother in a skin tent, or tupek, and in winter in a snow igloo, or iglooweuk.

Pomiuk's mother cooked the food over the usual stone lamp, which also served to heat their igloo in winter. This lamp, which was referred to in an earlier chapter, and described as a hollowed stone in the form of a half moon, was an exceedingly crude affair, measuring eighteen inches long on its straight side and nine inches broad at its widest part. When it was filled with oil squeezed from a piece of seal blubber, the blubber was suspended over it at the back that the heat, when the wick of moss was lighted, would cause the blubber oil to continue to drip and keep the lamp supplied with oil. The lamp gave forth a smoky, yellow flame. This was the only fireside that little Pomiuk knew. You and I would not think it a very cheerful one, perhaps, but Pomiuk was accustomed to cold and he looked upon it as quite comfortable and cheerful enough.

Ka-i-a-chou-ouk, Pomiuk's father, was a hunter and fisherman, as are all the Eskimos. He moved his tupek in summer, or built his igloo of blocks of snow in winter, wherever hunting and fishing were the best, but always close to the sea.

Here, under the shadow of mighty cliffs and towering, rugged mountains, by the side of the great water, Pomiuk was born and grew into young boyhood, and played and climbed among the mountain crags or along the ocean shore with other boys. He loved the rugged, naked mountains, they stood so firm and solid! No storm or gale could ever make them afraid, or weaken them. Always they were the same, towering high into the heavens, untrod and unchanged by man, just as they had stood facing the arctic storms through untold ages.

From the high places he could look out over the sea, where icebergs glistened in the sunshine, and sometimes he could see the sail of a fishing schooner that had come out of the mysterious places beyond the horizon. He loved the sea. Day and night in summer the sound of surf pounding ceaselessly upon the cliffs was in his ears. It was music to him, and his lullaby by night.

But he loved the sea no less in winter when it lay frozen and silent and white. As far as his vision reached toward the rising sun, the endless plain of ice stretched away to the misty place where the ice and sky met. Pomiuk thought it would be a fine adventure, some night, when he was grown to be a man and a great hunter, to take the dogs and komatik and drive out over the ice to the place from which the sun rose, and be there in the morning to meet him. He had no doubt the sun rose out of a hole in the ice, and it did not seem so far away.

Pomiuk's world was filled with beautiful and wonderful things. He loved the bright flowers that bloomed under the cliffs when the winter snows were gone, and the brilliant colors that lighted the sky and mountains and sea, when the sun set of evenings. He loved the mists, and the mighty storms that sent the sea rolling in upon the cliffs in summer. He never ceased to marvel at the aurora borealis, which by night flashed over the heavens in wondrous streams of fire and lighted the darkened world. His father told him the aurora borealis was the spirits of their departed people dancing in the sky. He learned the ways of the wild things in sea and on land and never tired of following the tracks of beasts in the snow, or of watching the seals sunning themselves on rocks or playing about in the water.

The big wolf dogs were his special delight. His father kept nine of them, and many an exciting ride Pomiuk had behind them when his father took him on the komatik to hunt seals or to look at fox traps, or to visit the Trading Post.

When he was a wee lad his father made for him a small dog whip of braided walrus hide. This was Pomiuk's favorite possession. He practiced wielding it, until he became so expert he could flip a pebble no larger than a marble with the tip end of the long lash; and he could snap and crack the lash with a report like a pistol shot.

As he grew older and stronger he practiced with his father's whip, until he became quite as expert with that as with his own smaller one. This big whip had a wooden handle ten inches in length, and a supple lash of braided walrus hide thirty-five feet long. The lash was about an inch in diameter where it joined the handle, tapering to a thin tip at the end.

One summer day, when Pomiuk was ten years of age, a strange ship dropped anchor off the rocky shore where Pomiuk's father and several other Eskimo families had pitched their tupeks, while they fished in the sea near by for cod or hunted seals. A boat was launched from the ship, and as it came toward the shore all of the excited Eskimos from the tupeks, men, women and children, and among them Pomiuk, ran down to the landing place to greet the visitors, and as they ran every one shouted, "Kablunak! Kablunak!" which meant, "Stranger! Stranger!"

Some white men and an Eskimo stepped out of the boat, and in the hospitable, kindly manner of the Eskimo Pomiuk's father and Pomiuk and their friends greeted the strangers with handshakes and cheerful laughter, and said "Oksunae" to each as he shook his hand, which is the Eskimo greeting, and means "Be strong."

The Eskimo that came with the ship was from an Eskimo settlement called Karwalla, in Hamilton Inlet, on the east of Labrador, but a long way to the south of Nachvak Bay where Pomiuk's people lived. He could speak English as well as Eskimo, and acted as interpreter for the strangers.

This Eskimo explained that the white men had come from America to invite some of the Labrador Eskimos to go to America to see their country. People from all the nations of the world, he said, were to gather there to meet each other and to get acquainted. They were to bring strange and wonderful things with them, that the people of each nation might see how the people of other nations made and used their things, and how they lived. They wished the Labrador Eskimos to come and show how they dressed their skins and made their skin clothing and skin boats, and to bring with them dogs and sledges, and harpoons and other implements of the hunt.

The white men promised it would be a most wonderful experience for those that went. They agreed to take them and all their things on the ship and after the big affair in America was over bring them back to their homes, and give them enough to make them all rich for the rest of their lives.

The Eskimos were naturally quite excited with the glowing descriptions, the opportunity to travel far into new lands, and the prospect of wealth and happiness offered them when they again returned to their Labrador homes. Pomiuk and his mother were eager for the journey, but his father did not care to leave the land and the life he knew. He decided that he had best remain in Labrador and hunt; but he agreed that Pomiuk's mother might go to make skin boots and clothing, and Pomiuk might go with her and take the long dog whip to show how well he could use it.

And so one day Pomiuk and his mother said goodbye to his father, and with several other Eskimos sailed away to the United States, destined to take their place as exhibits at the great World's Fair in Chicago.

The suffering of the Eskimos in the strange land to which they were taken was terrible. In Labrador they lived in the open, breathing God's fresh air. In Chicago they were housed in close and often poorly ventilated quarters. The heat was unbearable, and through all the long hours of day and night when they were on exhibition they were compelled to wear their heavy winter skin or fur clothing. They were unaccustomed to the food. Some of them died, and the white men buried them with little more thought or ceremony than was given those of their dogs that died.

Pomiuk, in spite of his suffering, kept his spirits. He loved to wield his long dog whip. It was his pride. Visitors at the fair pitched nickles and dimes into the enclosure where the Eskimos and their exhibits were kept. Pomiuk with the tip of his thirty-five foot lash would clip the coins, and laugh with delight, for every coin he clipped was to be his. He was the life of the Eskimo exhibit. Visitors could always distinguish his ringing laugh. He was always smiling.

The white men who had induced the Eskimos to leave their homes failed to keep their promise when the fair closed. The poor Eskimos were abandoned in a practically penniless condition and no means was provided to return them to their homes. To add to the distress of Pomiuk's mother, Pomiuk fell and injured his hip. Proper surgical treatment was not supplied, the injury, because of this neglect, did not heal, and Pomiuk could no longer run about or walk or even stand upon his feet.

Those of the Eskimos who survived the heat and unaccustomed climate, in some manner, God alone knows how, found their way to Newfoundland. Pomiuk, in his mother's care, was among them. The hospitality of big hearted fishermen of Newfoundland, who sheltered and fed the Eskimos in their cabins, kept them through the winter. It was a period of intense suffering for poor little Pomiuk, whose hip constantly grew worse.

When summer came again, Doctor Frederick Cook, the explorer, bound to the Arctic on an exploring expedition, heard of the stranded Eskimos, and carried some of them to their Labrador homes on his ship; and when the schooners of the great fishing fleets sailed north, kindly skippers made room aboard their little craft for others of the destitute Eskimos. Thus Pomiuk, once so active and happy, now a helpless cripple, found his way back on a fishing schooner to Labrador.

We can understand, perhaps, the joy and hope with which Pomiuk looked again upon the rock-bound coast that he loved so well. Onthese shores he had lived care-free and happy and full of bounding health until the deceitful white men had lured him away. He had no doubt that once again in his own native land and among his own people in old familiar surroundings, he would soon get well and be as strong as ever he had been to run over the rocks and to help his father with the dogs and traps and at the fishing.

Pomiuk could scarcely wait to meet his father. He laughed and chattered eagerly of the good times he and his father would have together. He was deeply attached to his father who had always been kind and good to him, and who loved him better, even, than his mother loved him.

Pomiuk's heart beat high, when at last, one day, the vessel drew into the narrow channel that leads between high cliffs into Nachvak Bay. He looked up at the rocky walls towering two thousand feet above him on either side. They were as firm and unchanging as always. He loved them, and his eyes filled with happy tears. Just beyond, at the other end of the channel, lay the broad bay and the white buildings of the Hudson's Bay Company's trading post, where his father used to bring him sometimes with the dogs in winter or in the boat in summer. What fine times he and his father had on those excursions! And somewhere, back there, camped in his tupek, was his father. What a surprise his coming would be to his father!

Pomiuk was carried ashore at the Post. Eskimos camped near-by crowded down to greet him and his mother and the other wanderers who had returned with them. It would be a short journey now in the boat to his father's fishing place and his own dear home in their snug tupek. What a lot of things he had to tell his father! And at home, with his father's help he would soon be well and strong again.

Then he heard some one say his father was dead. Dazed with grief he was taken to one of the Eskimo tupeks where he was to make his home. All that day and for days afterward, days of deep, unspoken sorrow, the thought that he would never again hear his father's dear voice was in his mind and forcing itself upon him. The world had grown suddenly dark for the crippled boy. All of his fine plans were vanished.

One day late that fall Dr. Grenfell found Pomiuk lying helpless and naked upon the rocks near the tupek of the Eskimo who had taken him in. The little lad was carried aboard the hospital ship. He was washed and his diseased hip dressed, he was given clean warm clothing to wear, and altogether he was made more comfortable than he had been in many months. Then, with Pomiuk as a patient on board, the ship steamed away.

Thus Pomiuk bade goodbye to his home, to the towering cliffs and rugged sturdy mountains that he loved so well, and to his people. The dear days when he was so jolly and happy in health were only a memory, though he was to know much happiness again. Perhaps, lying helpless upon the deck of the hospital ship, he shed a tear as he recalled the fine trips he used to have when his father took him to the post with dogs and komatik in winter, or he and his father went cruising in the boat along the coast in summer. And now he would never see his dear father again, and could never be a great hunter like his father, as he had once dreamed he would be.

But the cruise was a pleasant one, with every moment something new to attract his attention. Dr. Grenfell was as kind and considerate as a father. Pomiuk had never known such care and attention. His diseased hip was dressed regularly, and had not been so free from pain since it was injured. Appetizing, wholesome meals were served him. Everyone aboard ship did everything possible for his comfort and entertainment.

Pomiuk was taken to the Indian Harbor Hospital where he remained until the cold of winter settled, and the hospital was closed for the winter season. Then he was removed to a comfortable home up the Bay. Under careful surgical treatment his hip improved until he was able to get about well on crutches.

There was never a happier boy in the world than this little Eskimo cripple in his new surroundings and with his new friends. He laughed and played about quite as though he had the use of his limbs, and had forgotten his affliction. During the winter one of the good missionaries from the Moravian Mission at Hopedale visited him and baptized him "Gabriel"—the angel of comfort. He was a comfort indeed and a joy to those who had his care.

XVI
MAKING A HOME FOR THE ORPHANS

The next winter Pomiuk was taken to the hospital at Battle Harbor where he could receive more constant surgical treatment. He was a joy to the doctors and nurses. His face was always happy and smiling. He never complained, and his amiable disposition endeared him not only to the doctors and nurses but to the other patients as well.

But Pomiuk was never to be well again. The diseased hip was beyond control, and was wearing down his constitution and his strength. One day he fell suddenly very ill. For a week he lay in bed, at times unconscious, and then early one morning passed away.

Many shed tears for Pomiuk when he was gone. They missed his joyous laughter and his smiling face. Doctor Grenfell missed him sorely. He could not forget the suffering, naked little boy that he had rescued from the rocks of Nachvak Bay, and he decided that some provision should be made to care for the other orphaned, homeless, neglected children of Labrador. In some way, he decided, the funds for such a home had to be found, though he had no means then at his disposal for the purpose. He further decided that the home must not be an institution merely but a real home made pleasant for the boys and girls, where they would have motherly care and sympathy, and where they should have a school to go to like the children of our own favoured land.

With cheerful optimism and heroic determination Doctor Grenfell set for himself the task of establishing such a home. And in the end great things grew out of the suffering and death of Gabriel Pomiuk. The splendid courage and cheerfulness of the little Eskimo lad was to result in happiness for many other little sufferers. Now, as always it was, with Doctor Grenfell, "I can if I will,"— none of the uncertainty of, "I will if I can." He pitched into the work of raising money to build that children's home. He lectured, and wrote, and talked about it in his usual enthusiastic way, and money began to come to him from good people all over the world. At length enough was raised and the home was built.

He had already picked up and taken into his mission family so many boys and girls, orphans or otherwise, that were without home or shelter, and that he could not leave behind him to suffer and die, that he had nearly enough on his hands to populate the new building before it was ready for them. Indeed he soon found himself almost in the position of the "old woman that lived in a shoe," and "had so many children she didn't know what to do." His big kind fatherly heart would never permit him to abandon a homeless child, and so he took them under his care, and somehow always managed to provide for them.

It was about the time of Pomiuk's death, I believe, that the first of these children came to him. One day, when cruising north in the Strathcona, he was told that a family living in an isolated and lonely spot on the Labrador coast required the attention of a doctor. He answered the call at once.

When he approached the bleak headland where the cabin stood, and his vessel hove her anchor, he was quite astonished that no one came out of the cabin to offer welcome, as is the custom with Labradormen everywhere when vessels anchor near their homes. He and his mate were put ashore in a boat, and as they walked up the trail to the cabin still no one appeared and no smoke issued from the stovepipe, which, rising through the roof, served as a chimney. When he lifted the latch he was quite decided no one, after all, was at home.

Upon entering the cabin a shocking scene presented itself. The mother of the family lay upon the bed with wide-open stare. Doctor Grenfell's practiced eye told him she was dead. The father, a Scotch fisherman and trapper, was stretched upon the floor, helplessly ill, and a hasty examination proved that he was dying. Five frightened, hungry, cold little children were huddled in a corner.

That night the father died, though every effort was made to revive him and save his life. Grenfell and his crew gave the man and woman as decent a Christian burial as the wilderness and conditions would permit, and when all was over the Doctor found five small children on his hands.

An uncle of the children lived upon the coast and this uncle volunteered to take one of them into his home. The other four Doctor Grenfell carried south on the hospital ship. There was no proper provision for their care at St. Anthony, his headquarters hospital, and he advertised in a New England paper for homes for them. One response was received, and this from the wife of a New England farmer, offering to provide for two. The Doctor sent two to the farm, the other two remaining at St. Anthony hospital.

The next child to come to him was a baby of three years. The child's father had died and the mother married a widower with a large family of his own. He was a hard-hearted rascal, and the mother was a selfish woman with small love for her baby. The man declined to permit her to take it into his home and she left it in a mud hut, a cellar-like place, with no other floor than the earth. A kind-hearted woman, who lived near by, ran in now and again to see the baby and to take it scraps of food and give it some care. She could not adopt it, for she and her husband were scarce able to feed the many mouths in their own family.

So alone this tiny little girl of three lived in the mud hut through the long days and the longer and darker nights. There was no mother's knee at which to kneel; no one to teach her to lisp her first prayer; no one to tuck her snugly into a little white bed; no one to kiss her before she slept. O, how lonely she must have been! Think of those chilly Labrador nights, when she huddled down on the floor in the ragged blanket that was her bed! How many nights she must have cried herself to sleep with loneliness and fear!

Here, in the mud hut, Doctor Grenfell found her one day. She was sitting on the earthen floor, talking to herself and playing with a bit of broken crockery, her only toy. He gathered her into his big strong arms and I have no doubt that tears filled his eyes as he looked into her innocent little face and carried her down to his boat.

In a locker on his ship, the Strathcona, there were neat little clothes that thoughtful children in our own country had sent him to give to the destitute little ones of Labrador. He turned the baby girl over to his big mate, who had babies of his own at home. The mate stroked her tangled hair with a brawney hand, and talked baby talk to her, and as she snuggled close in his fatherly arms, he carried her below decks. The baby's mother would not have known her little daughter if, two hours later, she had gone aboard the Strathcona and heard the peals of laughter and seen the happy little thing, bathed, dressed in neat clean clothes, and well fed, playing on deck with a pretty doll that Doctor Grenfell had somewhere found.

It was on his last cruise south late one fall, and not long before navigation closed, that Doctor Grenfell learned that a family of liveyeres encamped on one of the coastal islands was in a destitute condition, without food and practically unsheltered and unclothed.

He went immediately in search, steaming nearly around the island, and discerning no sign of life he had decided that the people had gone, when a little curl of smoke rising from the center of the island caught his eye. He at once brought his vessel to, let go the anchor, lowered away a boat and accompanied by his mate pulled ashore. Making the boat fast the two men scrambled up the rocks and set out in the direction from which they had seen the smoke rise.

Near the center of the island they suddenly brought up before a cliff, against which, supported by poles, was stretched a sheet of old canvas, pieced out by bits of matting and bagging, to form the roof of a lean-to shelter. In front of the lean-to a fire burned, and under the shelter by the fire sat a scantily clad, bedraggled woman. In her arms she held a bundle of rags, which proved to envelop a tiny new born baby, nursing at her breast.

A little girl of five, barefooted and ragged, slunk timidly back as the strangers approached. The woman grunted a greeting, but did not rise.

"Where is your man?" asked Doctor Grenfell.

"He's right handy, huntin' gulls," she answered.

Upon inquiry it was learned that there were three boys in the family and that they were also "somewheres handy about." A search discovered two of them, lads of seven and eight, practically naked, but tough as little bears, feeding upon wild berries. Their bodies were tanned brown by sun and wind, and streaked and splotched with the blue and red stain of berry juice. They were jabbering contentedly and both were as plump and happy in their foraging as a pair of young cubs.

Snow had begun to fall before Doctor Grenfell followed by the two lads returned to the fire at the cliff, soon to be joined by the boys' father, tall, gaunt and bearded. His hair, untrimmed for many weeks, was long and snarled. He was nearly barefooted and his clothing hung in tatters. In one hand he carried a rusty old trade gun, (a single-barreled, old-fashioned muzzle loading shotgun), in the other he clutched by its wing a gull that he had recently shot. Following the father came an older lad, perhaps fourteen years of age, little better clothed than his two brothers and as wild and unkempt in appearance as the father.

"Evenin'," greeted the man, as he leaned his gun against the cliff and dropped the gull by its side.

It was cold. The now thickly falling snow spoke loudly of the Arctic winter so near at hand. The liveyere and his family, however, seemed not to feel or mind the chill in the least, and apparently gave no more thought to the morrow or the coming winter, upon whose frigid threshold they stood, than did the white-winged gulls flying low over the water.

Fresh wood was placed upon the fire, and Grenfell and the mate joined the family circle around the blaze.

"Do you kill much game here on the island?" asked Doctor Grenfell.

"One gull is all I gets today," announced the man. "They bides too far out. I has no shot. I uses pebbles for shot, and 'tis hard to hit un with pebbles. 'Tis wonderful hard to knock un down with no shot."

"What have you to eat?" inquired the Doctor. "Have you any provisions on hand?"

"All us has is the gull," the man glanced toward the limp bird. "We eats berries."

"'Tis the Gover'me't's place to give us things," broke in the woman in a high key. "The Gov'me't don't give us no flour and nothin'."

"It's snowing and the berries will soon be covered," suggested Grenfell. "You can't live without something to eat and now winter is coming you'll need a house to live in. You haven't even a tent."

"Us would make out and the Gover'me't gave us a bit o' flour and tea and some clodin' (clothing)," harped the woman. "The Gover'me't don't give un to us. The Gover'me't folks don't care what becomes o' we."

"How are you going to take care of these children this winter?" asked Grenfell. "You can't feed them and without clothing they'll freeze. Let us take them with us. We'll give them plenty to eat and clothe them well."

"Don't be sayin' now you'll let un go!" broke in the mother in a high voice, turning to the man, who stood mute. "Don't be givin' away your own flesh and blood now! Don't let un go."

"You can't keep yourselves and these children alive through the winter. Some of you will starve or freeze," persisted Grenfell. "Suppose you let us have the two young lads and the little maid. We'll take good care of them and we'll give you some clothing we have aboard the vessel, and some flour and tea to start you."

"And a bit o' shot for my gun?" asked the man, showing interest.

"Don't be givin' away your own flesh and blood!" interjected the woman in the same high key. "'Tis the Gov'me't's place to be givin' us what we needs, clodin' and grub too."

"I'll let you have one o' th' lads and you lets me have a bit o' shot," the man compromised.

The sympathetic mate, with no intention of giving the man an opportunity to change his mind, seized the naked boy nearest him, tucked the lad, kicking and struggling, under one arm, and started for the boat, but upon Doctor Grenfell's suggestion waited, with the lad still under his arm, for developments.

In the beginning, to be sure, Doctor Grenfell had intended to issue supplies to the man, whether or no. But no matter how much or what supplies were issued there was no doubt these people would be reduced to severe suffering before summer came again. He wished to save the children from want, and to give them a chance to make good in the world as he believed they would with opportunity.

The oldest boy could be of assistance to his father in the winter hunting, and he could scarce expect the mother to give up her new-born baby. Therefore negotiations were confined to a view of securing the two small boys and the little girl.

Presently, in spite of violent protests from the mother, the father was moved, by promises of additional supplies, to consent to Grenfell taking the other boy. And immediately the man had said, "Take un both," the mate seized the second lad and with a youngster struggling under each arm, and with four bare legs kicking in a wild but vain effort for freedom and two pairs of lusty young lungs howling rebellion, he strode exultantly away through the falling snow to the boat with his captives.

No arguments and no amount of promised stores could move the father to open his mouth again, and Grenfell was finally compelled to be content with the two boys and to leave the little girl behind him to face the hardships and rigors of a northern winter. Poor little thing! She did not realize the wonderful opportunity her parents had denied her.

When negotiations were ended Doctor Grenfell arranged for the liveyeres to occupy a comfortable cabin on the mainland. He conspired with the agent of the Hudson's Bay Company, with the result that they were properly clothed and provisioned, a better gun was found for the man and an ample supply of ammunition.

Hundreds of stories might be told of the destitute little ones that have been, since the day he found Pomiuk on the rocks of Nochvak, gathered together by Doctor Grenfell and tenderly cared for in the Children's Home that was built at St. Anthony. There was a little girl whose feet were so badly frozen that her father had to chop them both off with an ax to save her life, and who Doctor Grenfell found helpless in the poor little cabin where her people lived. I wish there was time and room to tell about her. He took her away with him, and healed her wounds, and fitted cork feet to her stumps of legs so that she could go to school and run around and play with the other children. Indeed, she learned to use her new feet so well that today, if you saw her you would never guess that her feet were not her real ones.

And there was a little boy whose father was frozen to death at his trapping one winter, a bright little chap now in the home and going to school.

These are but a few of the many, many children that have been made happy and have been trained at the Home and under Doctor Grenfell's care to useful lives. Some of them have worked their way through college. Some of the boys served in the Great War at the front. Many are holding positions of importance. Let us see, however, what became of those particular ones, mentioned in this chapter.

One of the Scotch trapper's daughters found by Doctor Grenfell in the lonely cabin when her mother lay dead and her father dying is a trained nurse. The others are also in responsible positions.

The baby of the mud hut is a charming young lady, a graduate of a school in the United States, and the successful member of a useful profession.

Both of the little naked boys taken from the island that snowy day are grown men now, and graduates of the famous Pratt Institute in Brooklyn, New York. One is a master carpenter, the other the manager of a big trading store on the Labrador coast.

Now, as I write, in the fall of 1921, the walls of a new fine concrete home for the children are under construction at St. Anthony, to be used in conjunction with the original wooden building which is crowded to capacity. Children of the United States, Canada, and Great Britain giving of their pennies made the new building possible. More money is needed to furnish it, but enough will surely be given for the homeless little ones of the Labrador must be cared for.

And so, in the end, great things grew out of the suffering and death of Gabriel Pomiuk, the little Eskimo lad. His splendid courage and cheerfulness has led to happiness for many other little sufferers.

XVII
THE DOGS OF THE ICE TRAIL

One of the most interesting features of Labrador life in winter is dog travel. The dogs are interesting the year round, for they are always in evidence winter and summer, but in the fall when the sea freezes and snow comes, they take a most important place in the life of the people of the coast. They are the horses and automobiles and locomotives of the country. No one can travel far without them.

The true Eskimo dog of Labrador, the "husky," as he is called, is the direct descendant of the great Labrador wolf. The Labrador wolf is the biggest and fiercest wolf on the North American continent, and the Eskimo dog of northern Labrador, his brother, is the biggest and finest sledge dog to be found anywhere in the world. He is larger and more capable than the Greenland species of which so much has been written, and he is quite superior to those at present found in Alaska.

The true husky dog of northern Labrador has the head and jawls and upstanding ears of the wild wolf. He has the same powerful shoulders, thick forelegs, and bristling mane. He does not bark like other dogs, but has the characteristic howl of the wolf. There is apparently but one difference between him and the wild wolf, and this comes, possibly, through domestication. He curls his tail over his back, while the wolf does not. Even this distinction does not always hold, for I have seen and used dogs that did not curl their tail. These big fellows often weigh a full hundred pounds and more.

Indeed these northern huskies and the wild wolves mix together sometimes to fight, and sometimes in good fellowship. Once I had a wolf follow my komatik for two days, and at night when we stopped and turned our dogs loose the wolf joined them and staid the night with them only to slink out of rifle shot with the coming of dawn.

One of my friends, an agent of the Hudson's Bay Company, was once traveling with a native Labradorman driver along the Labrador coast, when his train of eight big huskies, suddenly becoming excited, gave an extra strain on their traces and snapped the "bridle," the long walrus hide thong that connects the traces with the komatik. Away the dogs ran, heading over a low hill, apparently in pursuit of some game they had scented.

My friend, on snowshoes, ran in pursuit, while the driver made a circuit around the hill in the hope of heading the dogs off. Ten minutes later the team swung down over the hill and back to the komatik. From a distance the men saw them and also turned back, but to their astonishment they counted not the eight dogs that composed their team, but thirteen. On drawing nearer they realized that five great wolves had joined the dogs.

The men's guns were lashed on the komatik, and both were, therefore, unarmed, and before they could reach the komatik and unlash the rifles the wolves had fled over the hill and out of range. The dogs, however, answered the driver's call and were captured.

One winter evening a few years ago I drove my dog team to the isolated cabin of Tom Broomfield, a trapper of the coast, where I was to spend the night. When our dogs were fed and we had eaten our own supper, Tom went to a chest and drew forth a huge wolf skin, which he held up for my inspection.

"He's a big un, now! A wonderful big un!" he commented. "Most big enough all by hisself for a man's sleepin' bag!"

"It's a monster!" I exclaimed. "Where did you kill it?"

"Right here handy t' th' door," he grinned. "I were standin' just outside th' door o' th' porch when I fires and knocks he over th' first shot."

"He were here th' day before Tom kills he," interjected Tom's wife. "He gives me a wonderful scare that wolf does. I were alone wi' th' two young ones."

"Tell me about it," I suggested.

"'Twere this way sir," said Tom, spreading the pelt over a big chest where we could admire it. "I were away 'tendin' fox traps, and I has th' komatik and all th' dogs, savin' one, which I leaves behind. Th' woman were bidin' home alone wi' th' two young ones. In th' evenin' her hears dogs a fightin' outside, and thinkin' 'tis one o' th' team broke loose and runned home that's fightin' th' dog I leaves behind, she starts t' go out t' beat un apart and stop th' fightin' when she sees 'tis a wolf and no dog at all. 'Twere a wonderful big un too. He were inside that skin you sees there, sir, and you can see for yourself th' bigness o' he.

"Her tries t' take down th' rifle, th' one as is there on th' pegs, sir. Th' wolf and th' dog be now fightin' agin' th' door, and th' door is bendin' in and handy t' breakin' open. She's a bit scared, sir, and shakin' in th' hands, and she makes a slip, and th' rifle, he goes off, bang! and th' bullet makes that hole marrin' th' timber above th' windy."

Tom arose and pointed out a bullet hole above the window.

"Then th' wolf, he goes off too, bein' scared at th' shootin'.

"I were home th' next day mendin' dog harness, when I hears th' dogs fightin', and I takes a look out th' windy, and there I sees that wolf fightin' wi' th' dogs, and right handy t' th' house. I just takes my rifle down spry as I can, and goes out. When th' dogs sees me open th' door they runs away and leaves th' wolf apart from un, and I ups and knocks he over wi' a bullet, sir. I gets he fair in th' head first shot I takes, and there be th' skin. 'Tis worth a good four dollars too, for 'tis an extra fine one."

They are treacherous beasts, but, like the wolf, cowardly, these big dogs of the Labrador. If a man should trip and fall among them, the likelihood is he would be torn to pieces by their fangs before he could help himself. You cannot make pals of them as you can of other dogs. They would as lief snap off the hand that reared and feeds them as not. It is never safe for a stranger to move among a pack of them without a stick in his hand. But a threatened kick or the swing of a menacing stick will send them off crawling and whining.

The Hudson's Bay Company once had a dozen or so of these big fellows at Cartwright Post, in Sandwich Bay. They were exceptionally fine dogs of the true husky breed, brought down from one of the more northerly posts, and the agent was proud of them. This was the same agent whose dogs ran away to chum with the wolves, and I believe these were some of the same dogs. They were splendid animals in harness, well broken and tireless travelers on the trail.

One evening, late in the fall, the agent's wife was standing at the open door of the post house, and her little boy, a lad of about your years, was playing near the doorstep.

Labrador dogs are fed but once a day, and this is always in the evening. It was feeding time for the dogs, and a servant down at the feed house, where the dog rations were kept, called them. With a rush they responded. Just when some of them were passing the post house the little boy in his play stumbled and fell. In an instant the dogs were upon him. The mother, with rare presence of mind, sprang forward, seized the boy, sprang back into the house and slammed the door upon the dogs.

The boy was on the ground but a moment, but in that moment he was horribly torn by the sharp fangs. At one place his entrails were laid bare. There were over sixty wounds on his little body. The dogs lapped up the blood that fell upon the ground and doorstep. That night the pack, like a pack of hungry wolves, congregated outside the window where they heard the child crying and moaning with pain and all night howled as wolves howl when they have cornered prey.

The following morning it happened providentially that Doctor Grenfell's hospital ship steamed into Cartwright Harbor and dropped anchor. The Doctor himself was aboard. He took the boy under his charge and the little one's life was saved through his skill.

After the attack the dogs became extremely aggressive and surly. They were like a pack of fierce wolves. No one about the place was safe, and the agent was compelled to shoot every animal in defense of human life. Usually in Labrador when dogs are guilty of attacking people they are hung by the neck to a gibbet until dead, and left hanging for several days. I have seen dogs thus hanging after execution.

When I left Davis Inlet Post of the Hudson's Bay Company with my dog team one cold winter morning, a native trapper told me that he would follow later in the day and probably overtake me at the Moravian Mission Station at Hopedale. We made half the journey to Hopedale that night and spent the night in a native cabin. A storm was threatening the next morning, but, nevertheless, we set forward. Shortly after midday the storm broke with a gale of wind and driving, smothering snow, and a temperature 30 degrees below zero. Every moment it increased in fury, but fortunately we reached the mission station before it had reached its worst, and here remained stormbound for two days, during which time the trapper did not appear.

Later I learned that, with his wife and young son he left Davis Inlet a few hours after our departure. After the storm had abated his dog team appeared at Davis Inlet, but he and his wife and child were not heard from. A searching party set out, but could find no trace of the missing ones.

In the spring, when the snow had begun to melt, the komatik was found and scattered about it were human bones. It was supposed that the man had halted to camp and await the passing of the storm. Benumbed by the cold he had probably fallen among his dogs, and they had torn him to pieces, and with whetted appetite had then attacked and killed his wife and child.

These great wolf dogs of the north are quite different from those of the south. It is doubtful if today a true Eskimo dog is to be found south of Sandwich Bay, and here and for a long distance north of Sandwich Bay many of the animals have mongrel blood in their veins. They are smaller and inferior. But from Sandwich Bay southward the difference is marked.

These southern dogs are faster, in a spurt of half a day or so, than the big wolf dog, but they lack size and strength, and therefore the staying powers that will carry them forward tirelessly day after day. The strain of wolf in their blood often makes them vicious, but in general they respond to kindly treatment and may be petted like dogs the world over, and sometimes the natives make house dogs of their leaders.

The dogs of Newfoundland, such as Doctor Grenfell uses in his winter journeys in going out from St. Anthony to visit patients, are still a different type. These are usually big lop-eared kindly fellows, and just as friendly as any dog in the world. The laws of Newfoundland provide a heavy fine upon any one bringing upon the island a Labrador dog that is related even remotely to the husky wolf dog.

The leader of the dog team is the best disciplined dog in the team but not always by any means the "boss" dog, or bully, of the pack. Every pack has its bully and generally, also, its under dog that all the others pick upon. Eskimo dogs fight among themselves, but the packs hold together as a gang against strange packs, and when sledges meet each other on the trail the drivers must exert their utmost effort and caution, and wield the whip freely, or there will be a fine mix-up, resulting often in crippled animals.

The komatik or sledge used in dog travel is from ten to fourteen feet in length, though in the far north I have seen them a full eighteen feet long. In the extreme north of Labrador, where the largest ones are found, they are but sixteen inches wide. Further south, in the region where the mission hospitals are situated, from ten to twelve feet is the usual length and about two feet the breadth.

In Alaska and the Northwest dogs are harnessed tandem, that is one in front of another in a straight line. This is a white man's method, and a fine method too when driving through timbered regions.

But in Labrador dog travel is usually on the naked coast and seldom in timbered country, and here the old Eskimo method is used. Each dog has its individual trace, which is fastened to the end of a single line of walrus skin leading from the komatik and called the bridle. The leading dog, which is especially trained to answer the driver's direction, has the longest trace, the next two dogs nearer the komatik shorter ones, the next two still shorter, and so on. Thus, when they travel the leader is in advance with the pack spread out behind him on either side, fan-shaped. Dogs follow the leader like a pack of wolves.

When the driver wishes the dogs to go forward he shouts "oo-isht," and to hurry "oksuit." If he wishes them to turn to the right he calls "ouk!", to the left "rah-der!", and to stop "Ah!"

In Newfoundland "Hist!" means "Go on"; "Keep off!" "to the right"; "Hold on!" "to the left." The dogs are harnessed in a similar manner to that used in Labrador, and the sledges are of the same form, though of the widest type.

When the dogs are put in harness in preparation for a journey they are always keen for the start. They will leap and howl in eagerness to be off unless the menace of a whip compels them to lie down. When the driver is ready he shouts "oo-isht!" to the dogs, as he pulls the nose of the komatik sharply to one side to "break" it loose from the snow. Immediately the dogs are away at a mad gallop, with the komatik swinging wildly from side to side. Quickly enough the animals settle down to a slow pace, only to spurt if game is scented or on approaching a building.

The usual dog whip is thirty or thirty-five feet in length, though I have seen them nearly fifty feet long. Eskimo drivers are exceedingly expert in handling the long whip, and in the hands of a cruel driver it is an instrument of torture. In southeastern and southern Labrador and in Newfoundland the dog whip is used much less freely than in the north, and the people are less expert in its manipulation than are the Eskimos. The different species of dogs renders the use of the whip less necessary.

Dog travel is seldom over smooth unobstructed ice fields. Sometimes it is over frozen bays where the tide has thrown up rough hummocks and ridges. I have been, under such conditions, nearly half a day crossing the mouth of a river one mile wide. Often the trail leads over high hills, with long hard steep climbs to be made and sometimes dangerous descents. In traveling over sea ice, especially in the late winter and spring, and always when an off shore wind prevails, there is danger of encountering bad ice, and breaking through, or having the ice "go abroad," and cutting you off from shore. When the tide has smashed the ice, it is often necessary to drive the team on the "ballicaders," or ice barricade, a narrow strip of ice clinging to the rocky shore. This is sometimes scarce wide enough for the komatik, and the greatest skill is necessary on the part of the driver to keep the komatik from slipping off the ballicader and falling and pulling the dogs into the sea.

When the snow is soft some one on snowshoes must go in advance of the dogs and pack the trail for them. Where traveling is rough, and in up-hill work, it is more than often necessary to pull with the dogs, and lift the komatik over obstructions.

In descending steep slopes the driver has a thick hoop of woven walrus hide, which he throws over the nose of one of the runners to serve as a drag. Even then, the descent may be rapid and exciting, and not a little dangerous for dogs and men. The driver throws himself on his side on the komatik clinging to it with both hands. His legs extend forward at the side of the sledge, he sticks his heels into the snow ahead to retard the progress, in imminent danger of a broken leg.

Winter settles early in Labrador and northern Newfoundland. Snow comes, the sea smokes, and then one morning men wake up to find a field of ice where waves were lapping the day before and where boats have sailed all summer.

Then it is that Doctor Grenfell sets out with his dogs and komatik over the great silent snow waste to visit his far scattered patients. Adventures meet him at every turn and some exciting experiences he has had, as we shall see.

XVIII
FACING AN ARCTIC BLIZZARD

The leader of Doctor Grenfell's dog team at St. Anthony, Newfoundland, is Gypsy, a big black and white fellow, friendly as ever a good dog can be, and trained to a nicety, always obedient and prompt in responding to the driver's commands. Running next behind Gypsy, and pulling side by side, are Tiger and Spider. Tiger is a large, good-natured red and white fellow, and Spider, his brother, is black and white. The next is Spot, a great white fellow with a black spot on his neck, which gives him his name. His mate in harness is a tawny yellow dog called Scotty. Then come Rover and Shaver. Rover is a small, black, lop-eared dog, about half the size of Shaver, who looks upon Rover as an inconsequent attachment, and though he thinks that Rover is of small assistance, he takes upon himself the responsibility of making this little working mate of his keep busy when in harness. Tad and Eric, the rear dogs, are the largest and heaviest of the pack, and perhaps the best haulers. Their traces are never slack, and they attend strictly to business.

This is the team that hauls Doctor Grenfell in long winter journeys, when he visits the coast settlements of northern Newfoundland, in every one of which he finds no end of eager folk welcoming him and calling him to their homes to heal their sick.

In the scattered hamlets and sparsely settled coast of northern Newfoundland the folk have no doctor to call upon at a moment's notice when they are sick, as we have. They live apart and isolated from many of the conveniences of life that we look upon as necessities.

It was this condition that led Doctor Grenfell to build his fine mission hospital at St. Anthony, and from St. Anthony, to brave the bitter storms of winter, traveling over hundreds of miles of dreary frozen storm-swept sea and land to help the needy, often to save life. He never charges a fee, but the Newfoundlander is independent and self-respecting, and when he is able to do so he pays. All that comes to Doctor Grenfell in this way he gives to the mission to help support the hospitals. Those who cannot pay receive from him and his assistants the same skilled and careful treatment as those who do pay. Money makes no difference. Doctor Grenfell is giving his life to the people because they need him, and he never keeps for his own use any part of the small fees paid him. He is never so happy as when he is helping others, and to help others who are in trouble is his one great object in life.

Two or three years ago the Newfoundland Government extended a telegraph line to St. Anthony. This offers the people an opportunity to call upon Doctor Grenfell when they are in need of him, though sometimes they live so far away that in the storms of winter and uncertainty of dog travel several days may pass before he can reach the sick ones in answer to the calls. But let the weather be what it may, he always responds, for there is no other doctor than Doctor Grenfell and his assistant, the surgeon at St. Anthony Hospital, within several hundred miles, north and west of St. Anthony.

Late one January afternoon in 1919 such a telegram came from a young fisherman living at Cape Norman, urging Doctor Grenfell to come to his home at once, and stating that the fisherman's wife was seriously ill. Grenfell's assistant had taken the dog team the previous day to answer a call, and had not returned, and if he were to go before his assistant's return there would be no doctor at the hospital. He therefore answered the man, stating these facts. During the evening another wire was received urging him to find a team somewhere and come at all costs.

It was evidently indeed a serious case. Cape Norman lies thirty miles to the northward of St. Anthony, and the trail is a rough one. The night was moonless and pitchy black, but Grenfell set out at once to look for dogs. He borrowed four from one man, hired one from another, and arranged with a man, named Walter, to furnish four additional ones and to drive the team. Walter was to report at the hospital at 4:30 in the morning prepared to start, though it would still be long before daybreak.

Having made these arrangements Grenfell went back to the hospital and with the head nurse called upon every patient in the wards, providing so far as possible for any contingency that might arise during his absence. It was midnight when he had finished. Snow had set in, and the wind was rising with the promise of bad weather ahead.

At 4:30 he was dressed and ready for the journey. He looked out into the darkness. The air was thick with swirling clouds of snow driven before a gale. He made out a dim figure battling its way to the door, and as the figure approached he discovered it was Walter, but without the dogs.

"Where are the dogs, Walter?" he asked.

"I didn't bring un, sir," Walter stepped inside and shook the accumulation of snow from his garments. "'Tis a wonderful nasty mornin', and I'm thinkin' 'tis too bad to try un before daylight. I've been watchin' the weather all night, sir. 'Tis growin' worse. We has only a scratch team and the dog'll not work together right 'till they gets used to each other. I'm thinkin' we'll have to wait 'till it comes light."

"You've the team to drive and you know best," conceded the Doctor. "Under the circumstances I suppose we'll save time by waiting."

"That we will, sir. We'd be wastin' the dogs' strength and ours and losin' time goin' now. We couldn't get on at all, sir."

"Very well; at daylight."

Walter returned home and Doctor Grenfell to his room to make the most of the two hours' rest.

It was scarce daylight and Walter had not yet appeared when another telegram was clicked in over the wires:

"Come along soon. Wife worse."

The storm had increased in fury since Walter's early visit. It was now blowing a living gale, and the snow was so thick one could scarce breathe in it. The trail lay directly in the teeth of the storm. No dogs on earth could face and stem it and certainly not the picked up, or "scratch" team as Walter called it, for strange dogs never work well together, and will never do their best by any means for a strange driver, and Walter had never driven any of these except his own four.

With visions of the suffering woman whose life might depend upon his presence, the Doctor chafed the forenoon through. Then at midday came another telegram:

"Come immediately if you can. Wife still holding out."

He had but just read this telegram when, to his astonishment, two snow-enveloped, bedraggled men limped up to the door.

"Where did you come from in this storm?" he asked, hardly believing his eyes that men could travel in that drift and gale.

"We comes from Cape Norman, sir, to fetch you," answered one of the men.

"Fetch me!" exclaimed the Doctor. "Do you believe dogs can travel against this gale?"

"No, sir, they never could stem it, not 'till the wind shifts, whatever," said the man. "Us comes with un drivin' from behind. The gale blows us here."

That was literally true. Ten miles of their journey had been over partially protected land, but for twenty miles it lay over unobstructed sea ice where the gale blew with all its force. Only the deep snow prevented them being carried at a pace that would have wrecked their sledge, in which case they would certainly have perished.

"When did you leave Cape Norman?" asked the Doctor.

"Eight o'clock last evenin', sir," said the man.

All night these brave men, with no thought of reward, had been enduring that terrible storm to bring assistance to a neighbor! After the manner of the Newfoundlanders they had already fed and cared for the comfort of their wearied dogs, before giving thought to themselves, staggering with fatigue as they were.

"Go into the hospital and get your dinner," directed the Doctor. "When you've eaten, go to bed. We'll call you when we think it's safe to start."

"Thank you, sir," and the grateful men left for the hospital kitchen.

It was after dark that evening when the two men again appeared at Doctor Grenfell's house. They were troubled for the safety of their neighbor's sick wife, and could not rest.

"Us were just gettin' another telegram sayin' to hurry, sir," announced the spokesman. "The storm has eased up a bit, and we're thinkin' to make a try for un if you're ready."

"Call Walter, and I'll be right with you," directed the Doctor.

"Us has been and called he, sir," said the man. "He's gettin' the dogs together and he'll be right here."

A lull in a winter storm in this north country, with the clouds still hanging low and no change of wind, does not promise the end of the storm. It indicates that this is the center, that it is working in a circle and will soon break upon the world again with even increased fury.

Doctor Grenfell knew this and the men knew it full well, but their anxiety for the suffering woman at Cape Norman would not permit them to sleep. Anything was better than sitting still. The decision to start was a source of vast relief to Doctor Grenfell, even though it were to venture into the face of the terrible storm and bitter cold. Grenfell will venture anything with any man, and if those men could face the wind and snow and cold he could.

In half an hour they were off. Before them lay the harbor of St. Anthony, and the ice must be crossed. Through the darkness of night and swirling snow they floundered down to it. The men were immediately knee-deep in slush and the two teams of dogs were nearly swimming. Their feet could not reach the solid bed of ice below. The immense weight of snow had pushed the ice down with the falling tide and the rising tide had flooded it.

The team from Cape Norman took the lead to break the way. Every one put on his snowshoes, for traveling without them was impossible. One of those with the advance team went ahead of the dogs to tramp the path for the sledge and make the work easier for the poor animals, while the other remained with the team to drive. In like manner Walter tramped ahead of the rear dogs and Doctor Grenfell drove them.

At length they reached the opposite shore, fighting against the gale at every step. Now there was a hill to cross.

Here on the lee side of the hill they met mighty drifts of feathery snow into which the dogs wallowed to their backs and the snowshoes of the men sunk deep. They were compelled to haul on the traces with the dogs. They had to lift and manipulate the sledges with tremendous effort. Up the grade they toiled and strained, yard by yard, foot by foot. Sometimes it seemed to them they were making no appreciable progress, but on they fought through the black night and the driving snow, sweating in spite of the Arctic blasts and clouds of drift that sometimes nearly stopped their breath and carried them off their feet.

The life of the young fisherman's wife at Cape Norman hung in the balance. The toiling men visualized her lying on a bed of pain and perhaps dying for the need of a doctor. They saw the agonized husband by her side, tortured by his helplessness to save her. They forgot themselves and the risk they were taking in their desire to bring to the fisherman's wife the help her husband was beseeching God to send. This is true heroism.

As the saying on the coast goes, "'tis dogged as does it," and as Grenfell himself says, "not inspiration, but perspiration wins the prizes of life." They finally reached the crest of the hill.

On the opposite or weather side of the hill the gale met them with full force. It had swept the slope clean and left it a glade of ice. They slid down at a dangerous speed, taking all sorts of chances, colliding in the darkness with stumps and ice-coated rocks and other snags, in imminent danger of having their brains knocked out or limbs broken.

The open places below were little better. Everything was ice-coated. They slipped and slid about, falling and rising with every dozen steps. If they threw themselves on the sledges to ride the dogs came to a stop, for they could not haul them. If they walked they could not keep their feet. Their course took them along the bed of Bartlett River, and twice Grenfell and some of the others broke through into the icy rapids.

At half past one in the morning they reached the mouth of Bartlett River where it empties into the sea and between them and Cape Norman lay twenty miles of unobstructed sea ice. They had been traveling for nearly six hours and had covered but ten miles of the journey. The temporary lull in the storm had long since passed, and now, beating down upon the world with redoubled fury, it met them squarely in the face. No dog could stem it. The men could scarce stand upright. The clouds of snow suffocated them, and the cold was withering.

Far out they could hear the thunder of smashing ice. It was a threat that the still firm ice lying before them might be broken into fragments at any time. Sea water had already driven over it, forming a thick coating of half-frozen slush. Even though the gale that swept the ice field had not been too fierce to face, any attempt to cross would obviously have been a foolhardy undertaking.

XIX
HOW AMBROSE WAS MADE TO WALK

One of the men from Cape Norman had been acting as leader on the trail from St. Anthony. His name was Will, and he was a big broad-shouldered man, a giant of a fellow. He knew all the trappers on this part of the coast, and where their trapping grounds lay. One of his neighbors, whom he spoke of as "Si," trapped in the neighborhood where the baffled men now found themselves.

"I'm rememberin', now, Si built a tilt handy by here," he suddenly exclaimed.

"A tilt!" Grenfell was sceptical. "I've been going up and down this coast for twenty years and I never heard of a tilt near here."

"He built un last fall. I thinks, now, I could find un," Will suggested.

"Find it if you can," urged Grenfell hopefully. "Where is it?"

"'Tis in a bunch of trees, somewheres handy."

"Is there a stove in it?"

"I'm not knowin' that. I'll try to find un and see."

They had retreated to the edge of the forest. Will disappeared among the trees, and Grenfell and the others waited. It was still six hours to daylight, and to stand inactive for six hours in the storm and biting cold would have been perilous if not fatal.

Presently Will's shout came out of the forest, rising above the road of wind:

"Ti-l-t and St-o-ve!"

They followed Will's voice, bumping against trees, groping through flying snow and darkness, and quickly came upon Will and the tilt. There was indeed, to their great joy, a stove in it. There was also a supply of dry wood, all cut and piled ready for use. In one end of the tilt was a bench covered with spruce boughs which Si used as a bed.

There was nothing to feed the exhausted dogs, but they were unharnessed and were glad enough to curl up in the snow, where the drift would cover them, after the manner of northern dogs.

Then a fire was lighted in the stove. Will went out with the ax and kettle, and presently returned with the kettle filled with water dipped from Bartlett River after he had cut a hole through the ice.

Setting the kettle on the stove, Will, standing by the stove, proceeded to fill and light his pipe while Doctor Grenfell opened his dunnage bag to get the tea and sugar. Suddenly Will's pipe clattered to the floor. Will, standing like a statue, did not stoop to pick it up and Grenfell rescued it and rising offered it to him, when, to his vast astonishment, he discovered that the man, standing erect upon his feet was fast asleep. He had been nearly sixty hours without sleep and forty-eight hours of this had been spent on the trail.

They aroused Will and had him sit down on the bench. He re-lighted his pipe but in a moment it fell from his teeth again. He rolled over on the bench and was too soundly asleep to be interested in pipe or tea or anything to eat.

Daylight brought no abatement in the storm. The ice was deep under a coating of slush, and quite impassable for dogs and men, and the sea was pounding and battering at the outer edge, as the roar of smashing ice testified, though quite shut out from view by driving snow. There was nothing to do but follow the shore, a long way around, and off they started.

Here and there was an opportunity to cut across small coves and inlets where the ice was safe enough, and at two o'clock in the afternoon they reached Crow Island, a small island three-quarters of a mile from the mainland.

Under the shelter of scraggly fir trees on Crow Island an attempt was made to light a fire and boil the kettle for tea. But there was no protection from the blizzard. They failed to get the fire, and finally compelled by the elements to give it up they took a compass course for a small settlement on the mainland. The instinct of the dogs led them straight, and when the men had almost despaired of locating the settlement they suddenly drew up before a snug cottage.

A cup of steaming tea, a bit to eat, and Grenfell and his men were off again. Cape Norman was not far away, and that evening they reached the fisherman's home.

The joy and thankfulness of the young fisherman was beyond bounds. His wife was in agony and in a critical condition. Doctor Grenfell relieved her pain at once, and by skillful treatment in due time restored her to health. Had he hesitated to face the storm or had he been made of less heroic stuff and permitted himself to be driven back by the blizzard, she would have died. Indeed there are few men on the coast that would have ventured out in that storm. But he went and he saved the woman's life, and today that young fisherman's wife is as well and happy as ever she could be, and she and her husband will forever be grateful to Doctor Grenfell for his heroic struggle to reach them.

In a few days Doctor Grenfell was back again in St. Anthony, and then a telegram came calling him to a village to the south. The weather was fair. His own splendid team was at home, and he was going through a region where settlements were closer together than on the Cape Norman trail.

The first night was spent in his sleeping bag stretched on the floor of a small building kept open for the convenience of travelers with dog sledges. The next night he was comfortably housed in a little cabin in the woods, also used for the convenience of travelers, and generally each night he was quite as well housed.

He was going now to see a lad of fifteen whose thigh had been broken while steering a komatik down a steep hill. Dog driving, as we have seen, is frequently a dangerous occupation, and this young fellow had suffered.

In every settlement Doctor Grenfell was hailed by folk who needed a doctor. There was one broken leg that required attention, one man had a broken knee cap. In one house he found a young woman dying of consumption. There were many cases of Spanish influenza and several people dangerously ill with bronchial pneumonia. There was one little blind child later taken to the hospital at St. Anthony to undergo an operation to restore her sight. In the course of that single journey he treated eighty-six different cases, and but for his fortunate coming none of them could have had a doctor's care.

He found the lad Ambrose suffering intense pain. After his accident the lad had been carried home by a friend. His people did not know that the thigh was broken, and when it swelled they rubbed and bandaged it.

The pain grew almost too great for the boy to bear. A priest passing through the settlement advised them to put the leg in splints. This was done, but no padding was used, which, as every Boy Scout knows, was a serious omission. Boards were used as splints, extending from thigh to heel and they cut into the flesh, causing painful sores.

The priest had gone, and though Ambrose was suffering so intensely that he could not sleep at night no one dared remove the splints. The neighbors declared the lad's suffering was caused by the pain from the injured thigh coming out at the heel.

Ambrose was in a terrible condition when Doctor Grenfell arrived. The pain had been continuous and for a long time he had not slept. The broken thigh had knit in a bowed position, leaving that leg three inches shorter than the other.

It was necessary to re-break the thigh to straighten it. Doctor Grenfell could not do this without assistance. There was but one thing to do, take the lad to St. Anthony hospital.

A special team and komatik would be required for the journey, but the lad's father had no dogs, and with a family of ten children to support, in addition to Ambrose, no money with which to hire one. A friend came to the rescue and volunteered to haul the lad to the hospital.

It was a journey of sixty miles. The trail from the village where Ambrose lived rose over a high range of hills. The snow was deep and the traveling hard, and several men turned out to help the dogs haul the komatik to the summit. Then, with Doctor Grenfell's sledge ahead to break the trail, and the other following with the helpless lad packed in a box they set out, Ambrose's father on snowshoes walking by the side of the komatik to offer his boy any assistance the lad might need.

The next morning Doctor Grenfell was delayed with patients and the other komatik went ahead, only to be lost and to finally turn back on the trail until they met Grenfell's komatik, which was searching for them.

The cold was bitter and terrible that day. The men on snowshoes were comfortable enough with their hard exercise, but it was almost impossible to keep poor Ambrose from freezing in spite of heavy covering. Now and again his father had to remove the moccasins from Ambrose's feet and rub them briskly with bare hands to restore circulation. He even removed the warm mittens from his own hands and gave them to Ambrose to pull on over the ones he already wore.

At midday a halt was made to "boil the kettle," and by the side of the big fire that was built in the shelter of the forest Ambrose was restored to comparative comfort. On the trail again it was colder than ever in the afternoon, and they thought the lad, though he never once uttered a complaint, would freeze before they could reach the cabin that was to shelter them for the night. At last the cabin was reached. A fire was hurriedly built in the stove, and with much rubbing of hands and legs and feet, and a roaring fire, he was made socomfortable that he could eat, and a fine supper they had for him.

At the place where they stopped the previous night Doctor Grenfell had mentioned that the oven that sat on the stove in this cabin, was worn out. One of the men immediately went out, procured some corrugated iron, pounded it flat with the back of an ax and then proceeded to make an oven for Grenfell to take with him on his komatik. Upon opening the oven now it was found that the good friend who had made the oven had packed it full of rabbits and ptarmigans, the white partridge or grouse of the north. In a little while a delicious stew was sending forth its appetizing odors. A pan of nicely browned hot biscuits, freshly baked in the new oven and a kettle of steaming tea completed a feast that would have tempted anyone's appetite, and Ambrose, for the first time in many a day relieved of much of his pain, through Doctor Grenfell's ministrations, enjoyed it immensely, and for the first time in many a night, followed his meal with refreshing sleep.

The next morning the cold was more intense than ever. Ambrose was wrapped in every blanket they had and, as additional protection, Doctor Grenfell stowed him away in his own sleeping bag, and packed him on the sledge. Off they went on the trail again. Late that afternoon they crossed a big bay, and St. Anthony was but eighteen mile away.

When Ambrose was made comfortable in a settler's cottage, Doctor Grenfell directed that he was to be brought on to the hospital the following morning, and he himself much needed at the hospital pushed forward at once, arriving at St. Anthony long after night.

But before morning the worst storm of the winter broke upon them. The buildings at St. Anthony rocked in the gale until the maids on the top floor of the hospital said they were seasick. And when the storm was over the snow was so deep that men with snowshoes walked from the gigantic snow banks to some of the roofs which were on a level with the drifts. Tunnels had to be cut through the snow to doors.

The storm delayed Ambrose and his friends, but after the weather cleared their komatik appeared. The lad was put on the operating table, the thigh re-broken and properly set by Doctor Grenfell, and the leg brought down to its proper length. Presently the time came when Grenfell was able to tell the father that, after all their fears, Ambrose was not to be a cripple and that he would be as strong and nimble as ever he was. This was actually the case. Doctor Grenfell is a remarkably skillful surgeon and he had wrought a miracle. The thankful and relieved father shed tears of joy.

"When I gets un," said he, his voice choked by emotion, "I'll send five dollars for the hospital."

Five dollars, to Ambrose's father, was a lot of money.

Winter storms, as we have seen, never hold Doctor Grenfell back when he is called to the sick and injured. Many times he has broken through the sea ice, and many times he has narrowly escaped death. The story of a few of these experiences would fill a volume of rattling fine adventure. I am tempted to go on with them. One of these big adventures at least we must not pass by. As we shall see in the next chapter, it came dangerously near being his last one.

XX
LOST ON THE ICE FLOE

One day in April several years ago, Dr. Grenfell, who was at the time at St. Anthony Hospital, received an urgent call to visit a sick man two days' journey with dogs to the southward. The patient was dangerously ill. No time was to be lost, for delay might cost the man's life.

It is still winter in northern Newfoundland in April, though the days are growing long and at midday the sun, climbing high now in the heavens, sends forth a genial warmth that softens the snow. At this season winds spring up suddenly and unexpectedly, and blow with tremendous velocity. Sometimes the winds are accompanied by squalls of rain or snow, with a sudden fall in temperature, and an off-shore wind is quite certain to break up the ice that has covered the bays all winter, and to send it abroad in pans upon the wide Atlantic, to melt presently and disappear.

This breaking up of the ice sometimes comes so suddenly that traveling with dogs upon the frozen bays at this season is a hazardous undertaking. Scarcely a year passes that some one is not lost. Sometimes men are carried far to sea on ice pans and are never heard from again.

A man must know the trails to travel with dogs along this rough coast. Much better progress is made traveling upon sea ice than on land trails, for the latter are usually up and down over rocky hills and through entangling brush and forest, while the former is a smooth straight-away course. When the ice is rotted by the sun's heat, however, and is covered by deep slush, and is broken by dangerous holes and open leads that cannot safely be crossed, the driver keeps close to shore, and is sometimes forced to turn to the land and leave the ice altogether. When the ice is good and sound the dog traveler only leaves it to cross necks of land separating bays and inlets, where distance may be shortened, and makes as straight a course across the frozen bays as possible.

There is a great temptation always, even when the ice is in poor condition, to cross it and "take a chance," which usually means a considerable risk, rather than travel the long course around shore. Long experience at dog travel, instead of breeding greater caution in the men of the coast, leads them to take risks from which the less experienced man would shrink.

These were the conditions when the call came that April day to Dr. Grenfell. Traveling at this season was, at best, attended by risk. But this man's life depended upon his going, and no risk could be permitted to stand in the way of duty. Without delay he packed his komatik box with medicines, bandages and instruments. It was certain he would have many calls, both for medical and surgical attention, from the scattered cottages he should pass, and on these expeditions he always travels fully prepared to meet any ordinary emergency from administering pills to amputating a leg or an arm. He also packed in the box a supply of provisions and his usual cooking kit.

Only in cases of stress do men take long journeys with dogs alone, but there was no man about the hospital at this time that Grenfell could take with him as a traveling companion and to assist him, and no time to wait for any one, and so, quite alone and driving his own team, he set out upon his journey.

It was mid-afternoon when he "broke" his komatik loose, and his dogs, eager for the journey, turned down upon the trail at a run. The dogs were fresh and in the pink of condition, and many miles were behind him when he halted his team at dusk before a fisherman's cottage. Here he spent the night, and the following morning, bright and early, harnessed his dogs and was again hurrying forward.

The morning was fine and snappy. The snow, frozen and crisp, gave the dogs good footing. The komatik slid freely over the surface. Dr. Grenfell urged the animals forward that they might take all the advantage possible of the good sledging before the heat of the midday sun should soften the snow and make the hauling hard.

The fisherman's cottage where he had spent the night was on the shores of a deep inlet, and a few rods beyond the cottage the trail turned down upon the inlet ice, and here took a straight course across the ice to the opposite shore, some five miles distant, where it plunged into the forest to cross another neck of land.

A light breeze was coming in from the sea, the ice had every appearance of being solid and secure, and Dr. Grenfell dove out upon it for a straight line across. To have followed the shore would have increased the distance to nearly thirty miles.

Everything went well until perhaps half the distance had been covered. Then suddenly there came a shift of wind, and Grenfell discovered, with some apprehension, that a stiff breeze was rising, and now blowing from land toward the sea, instead of from the sea toward the land as it had done when he started early in the morning from the fisherman's cottage. Still the ice was firm enough, and in any case there was no advantage to be had by turning back, for he was as near one shore as the other.

Already the surface of the ice, which, with several warm days, had become more or less porous and rotten, was covered with deep slush. The western sky was now blackened by heavy wind clouds, and with scarce any warning the breeze developed into a gale. Forcing his dogs forward at their best pace, while he ran by the side of the komatik, he soon put another mile behind him. Before him the shore loomed up, and did not seem far away. But every minute counted. It was evident the ice could not stand the strain of the wind much longer.

Presently one of Grenfell's feet went through where slush covered an opening crack. He shouted at the dogs, but, buffeted by wind and floundering through slush, they could travel no faster though they made every effort to do so, for they, no less perhaps than their master, realized the danger that threatened them.

Then, suddenly, the ice went asunder, not in large pans as it would have done earlier in the winter when it was stout and hard, but in a mass of small pieces, with only now and again a small pan.

Grenfell and the dogs found themselves floundering in a sea of slush ice that would not bear their weight. The faithful dogs had done their best, but their best had not been good enough. With super-human effort Grenfell managed to cut their traces and set them free from the komatik, which was pulling them down. Even now, with his own life in the gravest peril, he thought of them.

When the dogs were freed, Grenfell succeeded in clambering upon a small ice pan that was scarce large enough to bear his weight, and for the moment was safe. But the poor dogs, much more frightened than their master, and looking to him for protection, climbed upon the pan with him, and with this added weight it sank from under him.

Swimming in the ice-clogged water must have been well nigh impossible. The shock of the ice-cold water itself, even had there been no ice, was enough to paralyze a man. But Grenfell, accustomed to cold, and with nerves of iron as a result of keeping his body always in the pink of physical condition, succeeded finally in reaching a pan that would support both himself and the dogs. The animals followed him and took refuge at his feet.

Standing upon the pan, with the dogs huddled about him, he scanned the naked shores, but no man or sign of human life was to be seen. How long his own pan would hold together was a question, for the broken ice, grinding against it, would steadily eat it away.

There was a steady drift of the ice toward the open sea. The wind was bitterly cold. There was nothing to eat for himself and nothing to feed the dogs, for the loaded komatik had long since disappeared beneath the surface of the sea.

Exposed to the frigid wind, wet to the skin, and with no other protection than the clothes upon his back, it seemed inevitable that the cold would presently benumb him and that he would perish from it even though his pan withstood the wearing effects of the water. The pan was too small to admit of sufficient exercise to keep up the circulation of blood, and though he slapped his arms around his shoulders and stamped his feet, a deadening numbness was crawling over him as the sun began to sink in the west and cold increased.

Though, in the end he might drown, Grenfell determined to live as long as he could. Perhaps this was a test of courage that God had given him! It is a man's duty, whatever befalls him, to fight for life to the last ditch, and live as long as he can. Most men, placed as Grenfell was placed, would have sunk down in despair, and said: "It's all over! I've done the best I could!" And there they would have waited for death to find them. When a man is driven to the wall, as Grenfell was, it is easier to die than live. When God brings a man face to face with death, He robs death of all its terrors, and when that time comes it is no harder for a man who has lived right with God to die than it is for him to lie down at night and sleep. But Grenfell was never a quitter. He was going to fight it out now with the elements as best he could with what he had at hand.

These northern dogs, when driven to desperation by hunger, will turn upon their best friend and master, and here was another danger. If he and the dogs survived the night and another day, what would the dogs do? Then it would be, as Grenfell knew full well, his life or theirs.

The dogs wore good warm coats of fur, and if he had a coat made of dog skins it would keep him warm enough to protect his life, at least, from the cold. Now the animals were docile enough. Clustered about his feet, they were looking up into his face expectantly and confidently. He loved them as a good man always loves the beasts that serve him. They had hauled him over many a weary mile of snow and ice, and had been his companions and shared with him the hardships of many a winter's storm.

But it was his life or theirs. If he were to survive the night, some of the dogs must be sacrificed. In all probability he and they would be drowned anyway before another night fell upon the world.

There was no time to be lost in vain regrets and indecision. Grenfell drew his sheath knife, and as hard as we know it was for him, slaughtered three of the animals. This done, he removed their pelts, and wrapping the skins about him, huddled down among the living dogs for a night of long, tedious hours of waiting and uncertainty, until another day should break.

That must have been a period of terrible suffering for Grenfell, but he had a stout heart and he survived it. He has said that the dog skins saved his life, and without them he certainly would have perished.

The ice pan still held together, and with a new day came fresh hope of the possibility of rescue. The coast was still well in sight, and there was a chance that a change of wind might drive the pan toward it on an incoming tide. At this season, too, the men of the coast were out scanning the sea for "signs" of seals, and some of them might see him.

This thought suggested that if he could erect a signal on a pole, it would attract attention more readily. He had no pole, and he thought at first no means of raising the signal, which was, indeed, necessary, for at that distance from shore only a moving signal would be likely to attract the attention of even the keenly observant fishermen.

Then his eyes fell upon the carcasses of the three dogs with their stiff legs sticking up. He drew his sheath knife and went at them immediately. In a little while he had severed the legs from the bodies and stripped the flesh from the bones. Now with pieces of dog harness he lashed the legs together, and presently had a serviceable pole, but one which must have been far from straight.

Elated with the result of his experiment, he hastily stripped the shirt from his back, fastened it to one end of his staff, and raising it over his head began moving it back and forth.

It was an ingenious idea to make a flagstaff from the bones of dogs' legs. Hardly one man in a thousand would have thought of it. It was an exemplification of Grenfell's resourcefulness, and in the end it saved his life.

As he had hoped, men were out upon the rocky bluffs scanning the sea for seals. The keen eyes of one of them discovered, far away, something dark and unusual. The men of this land never take anything for granted. It is a part of the training of the woodsman and seaman to identify any unusual movement or object, or to trace any unusual sound, before he is satisfied to let it pass unheeded. Centering his attention upon the distant object the man distinguished a movement back and forth. Nothing but a man could make such a movement he knew, and he also knew that any man out there was in grave danger. He called some other fishermen, manned a boat and Dr. Grenfell and his surviving dogs were rescued.

XXI
WRECKED AND ADRIFT

It happened that it was necessary for Dr. Grenfell to go to New York one spring three or four years ago. Men interested in raising funds to support the Labrador and Newfoundland hospitals were to hold a meeting, and it was essential that he attend the meeting and tell them of the work on the coast, and what he needed to carry it on.

This meeting was to have been held in May, and to reach New York in season to attend it Dr. Grenfell decided to leave St. Anthony Hospital, where he then was, toward the end of April, for in any case traveling would be slow.

It was his plan to travel northward, by dog team, to the Straits of Belle Isle, thence westward along the shores, and finally southward, down the western coast of Newfoundland, to Port Aux Basque, from which point a steamer would carry him over to North Sydney, in Nova Scotia. There he could get a train and direct railway connections to New York. There is an excellent, and ordinarily, at this season, an expeditious route for dog travel down the western coast of Newfoundland, and Grenfell anticipated no difficulties.

Just as he was ready to start a blizzard set in with a northeast gale, and smash! went the ice. This put an end to dog travel. There was but one alternative, and that was by boat. Traveling along the coast in a small boat is pretty exciting and sometimes perilous when you have to navigate the boat through narrow lanes of water, with land ice on one side and the big Arctic ice pack on the other, and a shift of wind is likely to send the pack driving in upon you before you can get out of the way. And if the ice pack catches you, that's the end of it, for your boat will be ground up like a grain of wheat between mill stones, and there you are, stranded upon the ice, and as like as not cut off from land, too.

But there was no other way to get to that meeting in New York, and Grenfell was determined to get there. And so, when the blizzard had passed he got out a small motor boat, and made ready for the journey. If he could reach a point several days' journey by boat to the southward, he could leave the boat and travel one hundred miles on foot overland to the railroad.

This hike of one hundred miles, with provisions and equipment on his back, was a tremendous journey in itself. It would not be on a beaten road, but through an unpopulated wilderness still lying deep under winter snows. To Grenfell, however, it would be but an incident in his active life. He was accustomed to following a dog team, and that hardens a man for nearly any physical effort. It requires that a man keep at a trot the livelong day, and it demands a good heart and good lungs and staying powers and plenty of grit, and Grenfell was well equipped with all of these.

The menacing Arctic ice pack lay a mile or so seaward when Grenfell and one companion turned their backs on St. Anthony, and the motor boat chugged southward, out of the harbor and along the coast. For a time all went well, and then an easterly wind sprang up and there followed a touch-and-go game between Dr. Grenfell and the ice.

In an attempt to dodge the ice the boat struck upon rocks. This caused some damage to her bottom, but not sufficient to incapacitate her, as it was found the hole could be plugged. The weather turned bitterly cold, and the circulating pipes of the motor froze and burst. This was a more serious accident, but it was temporarily repaired while Grenfell bivouaced ashore, sleeping at night under the stars with a bed of juniper boughs for a mattress and an open fire to keep him warm.

Ice now blocked the way to the southward, though open leads of water to the northward offered opportunity to retreat, and, with the motor boat in a crippled condition, it was decided to return to St. Anthony and make an attempt, with fresh equipment, to try a route through the Straits of Belle Isle.

They were still some miles from St. Anthony when they found it necessary to abandon the motor boat in one of the small harbor settlements. Leaving it in charge of the people, Grenfell borrowed a small rowboat. Rowing the small boat through open lanes and hauling it over obstructing ice pans they made slow progress and the month of May was nearing its close when one day the pack suddenly drove in upon them.

They were fairly caught. Ice surrounded them on every side. The boat was in imminent danger of being crushed before they realized their danger. Grenfell and his companion sprang from the boat to a pan, and seizing the prow of the boat hauled upon it with the energy of desperation. They succeeded in raising the prow upon the ice, but they were too late. The edge of the ice was high and the pans were moving rapidly, and to their chagrin they heard a smashing and splintering of wood, and the next instant were aware that the stern of the boat had been completely bitten off and that they were adrift on an ice pan, cut off from the land by open water.

An inspection of the boat proved that it was wrecked beyond repair. All of the after part had been cut off and ground to pulp between the ice pans. In the distance, to the westward, rose the coast, a grim outline of rocky bluffs. Between them and the shore the sea was dotted with pans and pieces of ice, separated by canals of black water. The men looked at each other in consternation as they realized that they had no means of reaching land and safety, and that a few hours might find them far out on the Atlantic.

In the hope of attracting attention, Dr. Grenfell and William Taylor, his companion, fired their guns at regular intervals. Expectantly they waited, but there was no answering signal from shore and no sign of life anywhere within their vision.

For a long while they waited and watched and signalled. With a turn in the tide it became evident, finally, that the pan on which they were marooned was drifting slowly seaward. If this continued they would soon be out of sight of land, and then all hope of rescue would vanish.

"I'll tell you what I'll do, now," suggested Taylor. "I'll copy toward shore. I'll try to get close enough for some one to see me."

To "copy" is to jump from one pan or piece of ice to another. The gaps of water separating them are sometimes wide, and a man must be a good jumper who lands. Some of the pieces of ice are quite too small to bear a man's weight, and he must leap instantly to the next or he will sink with the ice. It is perilous work at best, and much too dangerous for any one to attempt without much practice and experience.

They had a boat hook with them, and taking it to assist in the long leaps, Taylor started shore-ward. Dr. Grenfell watched him anxiously as he sprang from pan to pan making a zigzag course toward shore, now and again taking hair-raising risks, sometimes resting for a moment on a substantial pan while he looked ahead to select his route, then running, and using the boat hook as a vaulting pole, spanning a wide chasm. Then, suddenly, Dr. Grenfell saw him totter, throw up his hands and disappear beneath the surface of the water. In a hazardous leap he had missed his footing, or a small cake of ice had turned under his weight.

XXII

SAVING A LIFE

It was a terrible moment for Grenfell when he saw his friend disappear beneath the icy waves. Would the cold so paralyze him as to render him helpless? Would he be caught under an ice pan? A hundred such thoughts flashed through Grenfell's mind as he stood, impotent to help because of the distance between them. Then to his great joy he saw Taylor rise to the surface and scramble out upon a pan in safety.

The ice was too far separated now for Taylor either to advance or retreat, and the pan upon which he had taken refuge began a rapid drift seaward. He had made a valiant effort, but the attempt had failed.

Grenfell resumed firing his gun, still hoping that some one might hear it and come to their rescue. Time passed and Taylor drifted abreast of Grenfell and finally drifted past him. Then, in the far distance, Grenfell glimpsed the flash of an oar. The flash was repeated with rhythmic regularity. The outlines of a boat came into view. The men shouted the good news to each other. Help was coming!

The signals had been heard, and in due time, and with much thankfulness, Dr. Grenfell and William Taylor were safely in the boat and on their way to St. Anthony.

Not long after his return to St. Anthony, the ice drifted eastward and an open strip of sea appeared leading northward toward the Straits of Belle Isle. The ice was now a full mile off shore, it was the beginning of June, and Dr. Grenfell, expecting that at this late season the Straits would be open for navigation, had the Strathcona made ready for sea at once, and with high hopes, stowed the anchor and steamed northward. It was his plan to have the vessel carry him westward through the Straits and land him at some port on the west coast of Newfoundland where he could take passage on the regular mail boat, which he had been advised had begun its summer service. Thence he could continue his trip to New York, where the important meeting had been adjourned several times in expectation of his coming.

But again he was doomed to disappointment. The Straits were found to be packed from shore to shore with heavy floe ice and clogged with icebergs. Before the Strathcona could make her escape she was surrounded by ice and frozen tight and fast into the floe.

Grenfell was determined to reach New York and attend that meeting. It was supremely important that he do so. Now there was but one way to reach the mail boat, and that was to walk. The distance to the nearest port of call was ninety miles.

Making up a pack of food, cooking utensils, bedding and a suit of clothes that would permit him to present a civilized and respectable appearance when he reached New York, he made ready for the long overland journey. Shouldering his big pack, he bade goodbye to Mrs. Grenfell, who was with him on the Strathcona, and to the crew, and set out over the ice pack to the land.

Three days later Dr. Grenfell reached the harbor where he was to board the mail boat upon her arrival. He was wearied and stiff in his joints after the hard overland hike with a heavy pack on his back, and looking forward to rest and a good meal, he went directly to the home of a mission clergyman living in the little village.

His welcome was hearty, as a welcome always is on this coast. The clergyman showered him with kindnesses. A pot of steaming tea and an appetizing meal was on the table in a jiffy. It was luxury after the long days on the trail and Grenfell sat down with anticipation of keen enjoyment.

At the moment that Grenfell seated himself the door opened unceremoniously, and an excited fisherman burst into the room with the exclamation:

"For God's sake, some one come! Come and save my brother's life! He's bleeding to death!"

Dr. Grenfell learned in a few hurried inquiries that the man's brother had accidentally shot his leg nearly off an hour before and was already in a comatose condition from loss of blood. The family lived five miles distant, and the only way to reach the cabin where the wounded man lay was on foot.

Grenfell forgot all about the steaming tea, the good meal and rest. A moment's delay might cost the man his life. Grenfell ran. Over that five miles of broken country he ran as he had never run before, with the half-frenzied fisherman leading the way.

The wounded man was a young fellow of twenty. Dr. Grenfell knew him well. He was a hero of the world war. He had volunteered when a mere boy, served bravely through four years of the terrible conflict and though he had taken part in many of the great battles he had lived to return to his home and his fishing.

"I never knew a better cure for stiffness than a splendid chance for serving," said Grenfell in referring to that run from the missionary's home to the fisherman's cottage. All his stiff joints and weary muscles were forgotten as he ran.

When Dr. Grenfell entered the room where the man lay, he found the young fisherman soaked with blood and sea water, lying stretched upon a hard table. The remnant of his shattered leg rested upon a feather pillow and was strung up to the ceiling in an effort to stop the flow of blood. He was moaning, but was practically unconscious, and barely alive.

The room was crowded to suffocation with weeping relatives and sympathetic neighbors. Dr. Grenfell cleared it at once. The place was small and the light poor and a difficult place in which to treat so critical a case or to operate successfully. He had no surgical instruments or medicines, and even for him, accustomed as he was to work under handicaps and difficulties, a serious problem confronted him.

The man was so far gone that an operation seemed hopeless, but nevertheless it was worth trying. Grenfell sent messengers far and near for reserve supplies that he had left at various points to be drawn upon in cases of emergency, and in a little while had at his command some opiates, a small amount of ether, some silk for ligatures, some crude substitutes for instruments, and the supply of communal wine from the missionary's little church, five miles away.

While these things had been gathered in, the flow of blood had been abated by the use of a tourniquet. There was scarcely enough ether to be of use, but with the assistance of two men Dr. Grenfell applied it and operated.

One of the assistants fainted, but the other stuck faithfully to his post, and with a cool head and steady hand did Dr. Grenfell's bidding. The operation was performed successfully, and the young soldier's life was saved through Dr. Grenfell's skillful treatment. Today this fisherman has but one leg, but he is well and happy and a useful man in the world.

Fate takes a hand in our lives sometimes, and plays strange pranks with us. In New York a group of gentlemen were impatiently awaiting the arrival of Dr. Grenfell, while he, in an isolated cottage on the rugged coast of Northern Newfoundland was saving a fisherman's life, and in the importance and joy of this service had perhaps for the time quite forgotten the gentlemen and the meeting and even New York.

Perhaps Providence had a hand in it all. If the water lanes had not closed, and the motor boat had not been damaged, and Dr. Grenfell and William Taylor had not been sent adrift on the ice, and no obstacles had stood in the way of Dr. Grenfell's journey to New York, and the Strathcona had not been frozen into the ice pack, in all probability this brave young soldier and fisherman would have died. There is no doubt that he believes God set the stage to send Dr. Grenfell on that ninety-mile hike.

XXIII
REINDEER AND OTHER THINGS

Hunting in a northern wilderness is never to be depended upon. Sometimes game is plentiful, and sometimes it is scarcely to be had at all. This is the case both with fur bearing animals and food game. So it is in Labrador. When I have been in that country I have depended upon my gun to get my living, just as the Indians do. One year I all but starved to death, because caribou and other game was scarce. Other years I have lived in plenty, with a caribou to shoot whenever I needed meat.

In Labrador the Eskimos and liveyeres rely upon the seals to supply them with the greater part of their dog feed, supplemented by fish, cod heads and nearly any offal. The Eskimos eat seal meat, too, with a fine relish, both cooked and raw, and when the seals are not too old their meat, properly cooked, is very good eating indeed for anybody.

The Indians rely on the caribou, or wild reindeer, to furnish their chief food supply, and to a large extent the caribou is also the chief meat animal of the liveyeres.

Sometimes caribou are plentiful enough on certain sections of the coast north of Hamilton Inlet. I remember that in January, 1903, an immense herd came out to the coast north of Hamilton Inlet, They passed in thousands in front of a liveyere's cabin, and standing in his door the liveyere shot with his rifle more than one hundred of them, only stopping his slaughter when his last cartridge was used. From up and down the coast for a hundred miles Eskimos and liveyeres came with dogs and komatik to haul the carcasses to their homes, for the liveyere who killed the animals gave to those who had killed none all that he could not use himself, and none was wasted.

That was a year of plenty. Oftener than not no caribou come within reach of the folk that live on the coast, and in these frequent seasons of scarcity the only meat they have in winter is the salt pork they buy at the trading posts, if they have the means to buy it, together with the rabbits and grouse they hunt, and, in the wooded districts, an occasional porcupine. Now and again, to be sure, a polar bear is killed, but this is seldom. Owls are eaten with no less relish than partridges, and lynx meat is excellent, as I can testify from experience.

But the smaller game is not sufficient to supply the needs and it occurred to Doctor Grenfell that, if the Lapland reindeer could be introduced, this animal would not only prove superior to the dog for driving, but would also furnish a regular supply of meat to the people, and also milk for the babies.

The domestic reindeer is a species of caribou. In other words, the caribou is the wild reindeer. The domestic and the wild animals eat the same food, the gray caribou moss, which carpets northern Newfoundland and the whole of Labrador, furnishing an inexhaustible supply of forage everywhere in forest and in barrens. The Lapland reindeer had been introduced into Alaska and northwestern Canada with great success. They would thrive equally well in Labrador and Newfoundland.

With this in mind Doctor Grenfell learned all he could about reindeer and reindeer raising. The more he studied the subject the better convinced he was that domesticated reindeer introduced into Labrador would prove a boon to the people. He appealed to some of his generous friends and they subscribed sufficient money to undertake the experiment.

In 1907 three hundred reindeer were purchased and landed safely at St.

Anthony, Newfoundland. With experienced Lapland herders to care for them they were turned loose in the open country. For a time the herd grew and thrived and the prospects for complete success of the experiment were bright.

It was Doctor Grenfell's policy to first demonstrate the usefulness of reindeer in Newfoundland, and finally transfer a part of the herd to Labrador. The great difficulty that stood in the way of rearing the animals in eastern Labrador was the vicious wolf dogs. It was obvious that dogs and reindeer could not live together, for the dogs would hunt and kill the inoffensive reindeer just as their primitive progenitors, the wolves, hunt and kill the wild caribou.

Because of the dogs, no domestic animals can be kept in eastern Labrador. Once Malcolm MacLean, a Scotch settler at Carter's Basin, in Hamilton Inlet, imported a cow. He built a strong stable for it adjoining his cabin. Twelve miles away, at Northwest River, the dogs one winter night when the Inlet had frozen sniffed the air blowing across the ice. They smelled the cow. Like a pack of wolves they were off. They trailed the scent those twelve miles over the ice to the door of the stable where Malcolm's cow was munching wild hay. They broke down the stable door, and before Malcolm was aware of what was taking place the cow was killed and partly devoured.

For generations untold, Labradormen have kept dogs for hauling their loads and the dogs have served them well. They were not willing to substitute reindeer. They knew their dogs and they did not know the reindeer, and they refused to kill their dogs. To educate them to the change it was evident would be a long process.

In the meantime the herd in Newfoundland was growing. In 1911 it numbered one thousand head, and in 1912 approximated thirteen hundred. Then an epidemic attacked them and numbers died. Following this, illegitimate hunting of the animals began, and without proper means of guarding them Doctor Grenfell decided to turn them over to the Canadian Government.

During those strenuous years of war, when food was so scarce, a good many of the herd had been killed by poachers. Perhaps we cannot blame the poachers, for when a man's family is hungry he will go to lengths to get food for his children, and Doctor Grenfell recognized the stress of circumstances that led men to kill his animals and carry off the meat. The epidemic, as stated, had proved fatal to a considerable number of the animals, and the herd therefore was much reduced in size. The remnant were corralled in 1918, and shipped to the Canadian Government at St. Augustine, in southern Labrador, where they are now thriving and promise marvelous results.

Some day Doctor Grenfell's efforts with reindeer will prove a great success at least in southern Labrador, where the dogs are less vicious, and play a less important part in the life of the people than on the eastern coast. Upon these thousands of acres of uncultivated and otherwise useless land the reindeer will multiply until they will not only feed the people of Labrador but will become no small part of the meat supply of eastern Canada. His introduction of reindeer into southern Labrador will be remembered as one of the great acts of his great life of activity. Their introduction was the introduction of an industry that will in time place the people of this section in a position of thrifty independence.

There never was yet a man with any degree of self-respect who did not wish to pay his own way in the world. Every real man wishes to stand squarely upon his own feet, and pay for what he receives. To accept charity from others always makes a man feel that he has lost out in the battle of life. It robs him of ambition for future effort and of self-reliance and self-respect.

Doctor Grenfell has always recognized this human characteristic. It was evident to him when he entered the mission field in Labrador that in seasons when the fisheries failed and no fur could be trapped a great many of the people in Labrador and some in northern Newfoundland would be left without a means of earning their living. There are no factories there and no work to be had except at the fisheries in the summer, trapping in winter and the brief seal hunt in the spring and fall. When any of these fail, the pantries are empty and the men and their families must suffer. But most of the people are too proud to admit their poverty when a season of poverty comes to them. They are eager for work and willing and ready always to turn their hand to anything that offers a chance to earn a dollar.

To provide for such emergencies Grenfell, many years ago, established a lumber camp in the north of Newfoundland, and at Canada Bay in the extreme northeast a ship building yard where schooners and other small craft could be built, and nearly everyone out of work could find employment.

In southern and eastern Labrador, where wood is to be had for the cutting, he arranged to purchase such wood as the people might deliver to his vessels. In return for the wood he gave clothing and other supplies.

Then came mat and rug weaving, spinning and knitting and basket making. Through Grenfell's efforts volunteer teachers went north in summers to teach the people these useful arts. He supplied looms. Every one was eager to learn and today Labrador women are making rugs, baskets and various saleable articles in their homes, and Grenfell sells for them in the "States" and Canada all they make. Thus a new means of earning a livelihood was opened to the women, where formerly there was nothing to which they could turn their hand to earn money when the men were away at the hunting and trapping.

Mrs. Grenfell has more recently introduced the art of making artificial flowers. The women learned it readily, and their product is quite equal to that of the

French makers.

Doctor Grenfell had been many years on the coast before he was married. Mrs. Grenfell was Miss Anna MacCalahan, of Chicago. Upon her marriage to Doctor Grenfell, Mrs. Grenfell went with him to his northern field. She cruises with him on his hospital ship, theStrathcona, acting as his secretary, braving stormy seas, and working for the people with all his own self-sacrificing devotion. She is a noble inspiration in his great work, and the "mother of the coast."

Doctor Grenfell has established a school at St. Anthony open not only to the orphans of the children's home but to all the children of the coast. There are schools on the Labrador also, connected with the mission. It is a fine thing to see the eagerness of the Labrador boys and girls to learn. They are offered an opportunity through Doctor Grenfell's thoughtfulness that their parents never had and they appreciate it. It is no exaggeration to say that they enjoy their schools quite as much as our boys and girls enjoy moving pictures, and they give as close attention to their books and to the instruction as any of us would give to a picture. They look upon the school as a fine gift, as indeed it is. The teachers are giving them something every day—a much finer thing than a new sled or a new doll—knowledge that they will carry with them all their lives and that they can use constantly. And so it happens that study is not work to them.

How much Doctor Grenfell has done for the Labrador! How much he is doing every day! How much more he would do if those who have in abundance would give but a little more to aid him! How much happiness he has spread and is spreading in that northland!

XXIV
THE SAME GRENFELL

Doctor Grenfell is not alone the doctor of the coast. He is also a duly appointed magistrate, and wherever he happens to be on Sundays, where there is no preacher to conduct religious services, and it rarely happens there is one, for preachers are scarce on the coast, he takes the preacher's place. It does not matter whether it is a Church of England, a Presbyterian, a Methodist, or a Baptist congregation, he speaks to the people and conducts the service with fine unsectarian religious devotion. Grenfell is a deeply religious man, and in his religious life there is no buncomb or humbug. He lives what he preaches. In his audiences at his Sunday services are Protestants and Roman Catholics alike, and they all love him and will travel far to hear him.

Norman Duncan, in that splendid book, "Doctor Grenfell's Parish," tells the story of a man who had committed a great wrong, amounting to a crime. The man was brought before Grenfell, as Labrador magistrate. He acknowledged his crime, but was defiant. The man cursed the doctor.

"You will do as I tell you," said the Doctor, "or I will put you under arrest, and lock you up."

The man laughed, and called Doctor Grenfell's attention to the fact that he was outside his judicial district, and had no power to make the arrest.

"Never mind," warned the Doctor quietly. "I have a crew strong enough to take you into my district."

The man retorted that he, also, had a crew.

"Are the men of your crew loyal enough to fight for you?" asked the Doctor. "There's going to be a fight if you don't submit without it. This is what you must do," he continued. "You will come to the church service at seven o'clock on Sunday evening, and before the whole congregation you will confess your crime."

Again the man cursed the Doctor and defied him. It happened that this man was a rich trader and felt his power.

The man did not appear at the church on Sunday evening. Doctor Grenfell announced to the congregation that the man was to appear to confess and receive judgment, and he asked every one to keep his seat while he went to fetch the fellow.

He found the man in a neighbor's house, surrounded by his friends. It was evident the man's crew had no mind to fight for him, they knew he was guilty. The man was praying, perhaps to soften the Doctor's heart.

"Prayer is a good thing in its place," said the Doctor, "but it doesn't 'go' here. Come with me."

The man, like a whipped dog, went with the Doctor. Entering the meeting room, he stood before the waiting congregation and made a complete confession.

"You deserve the punishment of man and God?" asked the Doctor.

"I do," said the man, no longer defiant.

The Doctor told him that God would forgive him if he truly repented, but that the people, being human, could not, for he had wronged them sorely. Then he charged the people that for a whole year none of them should speak or deal with that man; but if he made an honest effort to mend his way, they could feel free to talk with him and deal with him again at the end of the year.

"This relentless judge," says Norman Duncan, "on a stormy July day carried many bundles ashore at Cartwright, in Sandwich Bay of the Labrador. The wife of the Hudson's Bay Company's agent examined them with delight. They were Christmas gifts from the children of the "States" to the lads and little maids of that coast. The Doctor never forgets the Christmas gifts." The wife of the agent stowed away the gifts to distribute them at next Christmas time.

"It makes them very happy," said the agent's wife.

"Not long ago," said Duncan, "I saw a little girl with a stick of wood for a dolly. Are they not afraid to play with these pretty things?"

"Sometimes," she laughed, "but it makes them happy just to look at them. But they do play with them. There is a little girl up the bay who has kissed the paint off her dolly!"

And so even the tiniest, most forlorn little lad or lass is not forgotten by Doctor Grenfell. He is the Santa Claus of the coast. He never forgets. Nothing, if it will bring joy into the life of any one, is too big or too small for his attention.

Can we wonder that Grenfell is happy in his work? Can we wonder that nothing in the world could induce him to leave the Labrador for a life of ease? Battling, year in and year out, with stormy seas in summer, and ice and snow and arctic blizzards in winter, the joy of life is in him. Every day has a thrill for him. Here in this rugged land of endeavor he has for thirty years been healing the sick and saving life, easing pain, restoring cripples to strength, feeding and clothing and housing the poor, and putting upon their feet with useful work unfortunate men that they might look the world in the face bravely and independently.

There is no happiness in the world so keen as the happiness that comes through making others happy. This is what Doctor Grenfell is doing. He is giving his life to others, and he is getting no end of joy out of life himself. The life he leads possesses for him no element of self-denial, after all, and he never looks upon it as a life of hardship. He loves the adventure of it, and by straight, clean living he has prepared himself, physically and mentally, to meet the storms and cold and privations with no great sense of discomfort.

Wilfred Thomason Grenfell is the same sportsman, as, when a lad, he roamed the Sands o' Dee; the same lover of fun that he was when he went to Marlborough College; the same athlete that made the football team and rowed with the winning crew when a student in the University—sympathetic, courageous, tireless, a doer among men and above all, a Christian gentleman.